proclamation 2

**Aids for Interpreting the
Lessons of the Church Year**

**lesser
festivals 2**

Saints' Days and
Special Occasions

John Boone Trotti

editors: Elizabeth Achtemeier · Gerhard Krodel · Charles P. Price

FORTRESS PRESS   PHILADELPHIA

COPYRIGHT © 1980 BY FORTRESS PRESS

Library of Congress Cataloging in Publication Data (Revised)

Main entry under title:

Proclamation 2.

Consists of 24 volumes in 3 series designated A, B, and C which correspond to the cycles of the three year lectionary plus 4 volumes covering the lesser festivals. Each series contains 8 basic volumes with the following titles: Advent-Christmas, Epiphany, Lent, Holy Week, Easter, Pentecost 1, Pentecost 2, and Pentecost 3.

CONTENTS: [etc.]—Series C: [1] Fuller, R. H. Advent-Christmas. [2] Pervo, R. I. and Carl III, W. J. Epiphany.—Thulin, R. L. et al. The lesser festivals. 4 v.

1. Bible—Homiletical use. 2. Bible—Liturgical lessons, English.

[BS534.5.P76]   251   79–7377

ISBN 0–8006–4079–9 (ser. C, v. 1)

8278D80   Printed in the United States of America   1–1394

Contents

Editor's Foreword

The earliest saints' days in the church were local celebrations, held to mark the "birthday" of the martyrs into the kingdom through their faithful deaths. Thus a letter of A.D. 156, from the church of Smyrna regarding its burned bishop Polycarp, reads, "We afterwards took up his bones . . . and laid them in a suitable place; where the Lord will permit us to assemble together, as we are able, in gladness and joy, to celebrate the birthday of his martyrdom for the commemoration of those that have already fought in the contest and for the training and preparation of those that shall do so hereafter." Only very gradually were the nonmartyred admitted to the calendar, and it was in the West that the days came to mark the burial of the saint rather than his "birthday" to glory—the typical historicizing tendency found in Western Christendom.

None of the Western feasts honoring Mary is older than A.D. 700, while the feasts of the apostles and evangelists are mostly late and of mixed origins. But all served to Christianize daily life, and while saints' days and lesser festivals have at times been subject to abuse, along with major feasts such as Christmas, their purpose was finely stated in that same letter about Polycarp: "[Some said we would] 'abandon the Crucified and begin to worship this man' . . . not knowing that it will be impossible for us either ever to forsake the Christ who suffered for the salvation of the whole world of the redeemed—suffered for sinners though he was faultless—or to worship any other. For him, being the Son of God, we adore, but the martyrs as disciples and imitators of the Lord we cherish as they deserve for their matchless affection towards their own King and Master. May it be our lot also to be found partakers and fellow disciples with them."

The author of this volume is librarian and professor of bibliography at Union Theological Seminary in Virginia. A native of North

Carolina, John Boone Trotti was educated at Davidson College, Union Theological Seminary in Virginia, and Yale University, where he received his M.A. in 1961 and his Ph.D. in Old Testament in 1964. He also holds a master's degree in library science from the University of North Carolina. He has taught at Yale, at Randolph-Macon Woman's College, at the Presbyterian School of Christian Education, and at Union Seminary. He was pastor of the Altavista Presbyterian Church, Virginia, from 1964 to 1968, and has served as president of the American Theological Library Association and as a member of the Stillman College Board of Trustees. He is a specialist in the writings of Thomas Wolfe. Dr. Trotti and his wife have three children.

Richmond, Va.   ELIZABETH ACHTEMEIER

The Presentation of Our Lord

FEBRUARY 2

Lutheran	Roman Catholic	Episcopal
1 Sam. 1:21–28	Mal. 3:1–4	Mal. 3:1–4
Heb. 2:14–18	Heb. 2:14–18	Heb. 2:14–18
Luke 2:22–40	Luke 2:22–40 or Luke 2:22–32	Luke 2:22–40

EXEGESIS

First Lesson: 1 Sam. 1:21–28. This is a portion of the sustained narrative of the childhood and call of Samuel (chaps. 1—3). Elkanah and Hannah were childless. While on their annual pilgrimage to sacrifice at Shiloh, Hannah prayed fervently for a child (1:10–11) and vowed that should she be given a son he would be dedicated to the Lord as a Nazirite. Nazirites were persons who were consecrated to God. Characteristic marks of their devotion were untrimmed hair and abstention from strong drink (cf. Num. 6). The birth of Samuel was the answer to prayer.

Apparently Elkanah intended to fulfill his wife's vows (cf. Num. 30) and to give over his son at the first annual feast. Although Judg. 21:19 mentions an annual feast at Shiloh (see also 1 Sam. 2:19), it is not clear whether this was an ancient festival preceding the three obligatory great festivals (Deut. 16:16) or simply Elkanah's own family custom, perhaps relating to an earlier vow (1:21). Hannah insisted on keeping Samuel until he was weaned, perhaps as much as two or three years. That the time of weaning occasioned great celebration may be seen in the case of Isaac (Gen. 21:8). At that time Hannah would bring her son to "appear before the Lord" (cf. Ps. 42:2).

For the consecration of Samuel, Hannah brought a three-year-old bull, fully matured and quite valuable; a bushel of flour; and ample

7

wine. The bull was slain as a sacrifice of expiation for the young child, who was then taken to the resident priest, Eli. Invoking a most solemn oath, "As you live . . ." (cf. 1 Sam. 14:39), Hannah reminds Eli of her prayer and her vow, then "lends" Samuel to the Lord. The word "lends" also means "gives" (Exod. 12:36), and surely an unreserved dedication is intended here (cf. 1:11).

The episode ends in 2:11, where after worship and Hannah's extended prayer Elkanah returned home. This verse leaves open the notion that Hannah might have stayed with Samuel to tend to him until he was older, although the Septuagint indicates that both Hannah and Elkanah returned home. In any event, with the characteristically Spartan language and description, we are given no insight into the emotional quality of this giving and its impact on the parents (cf. Abraham's near sacrifice of Isaac in Gen. 22, which is rendered without psychological comment).

The Roman Catholic First Lesson is Mal. 3:1–4. That text is the Lutheran First Lesson for the Nativity of St. John the Baptist, for which there is discussion below.

Second Lesson: Heb. 2:14–18. The Book of Hebrews takes on the difficult question of the incarnation and the person of Jesus, not in the abstract, but in specific reference to his priestly sacrifice which fulfills and culminates all sacrificial requirements. As background one should give careful attention to the role of the high priest, the nature of sacrifices, and the Day of Atonement (cf. Lev. 16). This Jesus "for a little while" (so Heb. 2:7, 9 render Ps. 8:5) has taken upon himself a complete identification with our sufferings, temptations, and mortality that he might be the perfect High Priest and sacrifice (cf. Heb. 4:14–16; Rom. 8:3; and Phil. 2:7).

In v. 14 this identification consists in Jesus' sharing our "flesh and blood" (cf. Matt. 16:17; 1 Cor. 15:50). This frailty of complete humanity leads to the threat of sin and death, which threat this High Priest conquers. First, the sacrificial work of Jesus destroys, or better "brings to naught" or "renders impotent," the devil. It was commonly accepted that the devil rules the kingdom of death and that the sting of death is sin (cf. 1 Cor. 15:54–57). The precise manner of the conquest of the devil is not expanded upon.

The second aim of this sacrifice of Christ is the conquest of the fear of death in mankind. Such fear is common to all humanity in all ages but takes particular focus in the OT as the separation from all characteristics of life and especially from God (cf. Ps. 6:5; Isa. 38:10–11). V. 15 uses the language of deliverance (a new "exodus") to express Christ's dealing with this fear of death. Paul described this same joyful liberation in Romans (see 6:17 and 8:21, as indeed much of Rom. 5—8).

Christ's superiority to the angels (cf. Heb. 1) is reaffirmed here. He is not concerned with "taking the hand" (cf. Jer. 31:32) to save divine beings in his divine nature, but rather has taken hold of "the descendants of Abraham," not Jews only but all humanity who have faith (cf. Heb. 11).

The crux of the matter comes in verses 17–18, where it is affirmed that it was necessary that Christ share our complete humanity in order to be the merciful and faithful High Priest. His perfect priesthood is contrasted with the imperfection of the Jewish high priest, who had first to atone for his own sins (Lev. 16; Heb. 7:26–28). This faithfulness is expanded upon later in chap. 3, and his mercy is discussed in chaps. 4 and 5. As the perfect High Priest he not only identifies with us and is able to empathize, but also he is able to "expiate" our sins—unlike the imperfect priest who cannot finally remove the obstacle to God. The term "expiate" refers to Christ's dealing with the blockage of sin, not with the pagan notion of "propitiating" an angry God. This perfect High Priest is effective in that he has shared in suffering and in temptation (being also tempted by and in sufferings), yet he has not yielded to them (Heb. 4:15).

Gospel: Luke 2:22–40. This climax of Luke's infancy narrative portrays Joseph and Mary as a pious Jewish family fulfilling all legal demands with regard to the firstborn child. The child has already been circumcised (Luke 2:21), and now the other two requirements are attended to: the presentation of the firstborn (Exod. 13:2, 12) and the purification of the mother (Lev. 12:2–8). There is some confusion of those two rites, perhaps because Luke stood outside of that tradition. Here both Mary and Joseph are purified as parents at the same time they present Jesus. The parents appear to be somewhat surprised that

Jesus is uniquely "holy to the Lord." There is a legal provision whereby a poor family could substitute the turtledoves and pigeons for the more costly sacrifice of a lamb (Lev. 12:8)—evidence that Jesus' family was of limited means.

The presentation of Jesus is the focal point and is highly reminiscent of the presentation of Samuel (above). Simeon, a righteous and devout man whose piety had not satisfied him but had led him to a burning expectancy for the coming gracious action of God, "the consolation of Israel" (Isa. 40ff.), was among those who, like Joseph of Arimathea, were "looking for the kingdom of God" (Luke 23:51). Led of the Holy Spirit, Simeon came to the temple and took up the child to bless him—a common practice.

Simeon utters his famous Nunc Dimittis (vv. 29–32), which sweet and solemn canticle has been used in evening services of the church since the fifth century. In this utterance Simeon beseeches the Lord (using slave/master terminology) now to "let him depart" or "set him free" in peace. Having been a watchman in the dark hours, he now sees in this child the Sun of hope rising as a light to the nations (Isa. 42:6 and 49:6). This interpretation of the mission of Jesus amazes Mary and Joseph, who are also blessed by Simeon. Simeon's words contain ominous overtones for Mary (vv. 34–35) indicating that her son will be controversial and that she will share in the suffering of his mission. Jesus will occasion the "fall and rising" of many, both in the obvious sense of being a stone of stumbling or offense (cf. Ps. 118:22; Isa. 8:14) and in the sense of causing his followers to be humbled before they would rise even as he would.

A second prophetic utterance is given by the prophetess Anna, who dwells in the temple precincts much as Huldah the prophetess before her (2 Kings 22:14). We learn of her devotion and thanksgiving for this child who fulfills her fervent hopes for one who will redeem Jerusalem (vv. 36–38). Her constant prayer and fasting may be likened to the perseverance of the widow in Luke 18:1–8. Whereas Simeon's response is expressed in fulfillment and readiness to die, Anna comes alive with joy and thanksgiving and busies herself with telling those who expect redemption that their hopes are realized.

The story ends with the parents' having fulfilled the ritual demands and received both blessing and threat with regard to their son's painful mission. Like John the Baptist before him (Luke 1:80), Jesus grew and was filled with wisdom and the favor of God (see also the description of Samson in Judg. 13:24 and especially of Samuel in 1 Sam. 2:26).

HOMILETICAL INTERPRETATION

In this festival our attention is turned from the warmth and beauty of the Christmas season to the cold and ugly prospect of Good Friday's cross. Christian symbolism has linked the manger and the cross, correctly understanding the perilous mission of the Babe of Bethlehem. Our texts are united in their parallel themes of expectancy, pious devotion, faithful exercise of the faith in the house of the Lord, and perception of the fulfillment of the hope for God's salvation.

First Lesson: 1 Sam. 1:21–28. There are clear parallels here to the Gospel account. A miraculous birth (a birth to a barren woman in her old age) comes as the answer to devoted prayer. Samuel's family is presented as completely faithful in prayer, regularity of worship, and fulfillment of vows. The giving up of this son who was such a great joy in their old age is an act of great devotion and unselfishness in the extreme. One may appropriately ponder the significance of vows and bargains made with the Lord—be very careful what you pray for, you may get it.

The preacher may reflect on the faith and dedication of this family in preparing the way for the child Samuel to engage in his significant prophetic ministry for the Lord. The prayers of faithful parents have prepared the way for many a young man or young woman to enter the ministry. Although for most this does not require giving the child up at such an early age, there is a sense in which one gives up a child for Christian service by releasing him or her from family roles or expectations, the family business or the like. Beyond the specific discussion of the family's dealing with the consecration of a child to holy orders, surely there is a model of steady piety in Hannah and Elkanah applicable to all. They embody those who find stability and meaning in life through prayer and regular religious devotion. Their fulfillment of these vows with regard to Samuel parallels the humble acquiescence

of Mary later when she is called to be the mother of another consecrated One.

The Malachi text emphasizes the notion of purification of the temple and of sacrifices. John will come as forerunner to prepare the way,
but the true purification will come in the judgment of Jesus' own
person, the culmination of all such sacrifices in his own sacrifice.

Second Lesson: Heb. 2:14-18. Here one sees more clearly the
meaning and the necessity of Christ's coming in the flesh. The high
priest of the old covenant identified with the people but was so locked
into the same weaknesses and sins of the people as not to be able to
effect reconciliation between God and his people. God's long-
expected salvation came in this Jesus, meaning "Yahweh is salvation." The constant threat and most common heresy for the early
church (and dare we say for the modern one?) was that of Docetism.
This was the conviction that God has come down to us, with angels
and all, to save and that surely his Christ could not be "common" like
us but was only divine. Just raise the issue of the sexuality of Jesus, or
that of his limited knowledge as man, and you will quickly get a gauge
of the spiritual temperature of the average congregation. No, the
major issue was whether he was truly man.

In popular, or serious, psychology we constantly press for understanding, for empathy, for knowing life as someone else has experi-
enced it. This has been caught quite well in the folk song "Walk a Mile
in My Shoes." It is caught in the ubiquitous fantasy and frequent
literary motif of somehow becoming invisible in order to enter the
world of others and to observe what is "really going on" when their
defenses are down. Our text affirms that it was necessary for our High
Priest to walk in our shoes, but not as an invisible one simply observ-
ing nor as God in a man's suit playing out a role. He shared our
humanity from the baby's cry in the manger through the blood, sweat,
tears, and trials of becoming truly man. He was tested in all ways as
we: knowing hunger, pain, loneliness, fear, the joy and threat of
sexual stirrings, laughter, manual labor, and the rest.

Yet there is a difference. He was identified with us to set us free.
This he does, not by striking out as Moses did in killing the Egyptian
when he cast his lot with the Hebrews (Exod. 2:11-12), but by living a

life of complete obedience—tempted in all ways, yet without sin. In this life and its culmination in sacrificial death, our High Priest is both priest and sacrifice. Here one may expand upon the way in which Jesus overcomes death, the devil, and the crippling fear of death in humankind.

Gospel: Luke 2:22–40. Again one sees the pious family going about the sacred family rituals. It is in the regular rounds of worship and in the context of the house of God that the family, parents and children, are blessed. Wouldn't a little quiet celebration at home have done it as well? Surely, preacher, we make too much of special buildings and holy rites.

And what of Simeon and Anna? Couldn't Simeon have carried his expectancy to the local library, or sporting arena? Couldn't Anna have dwelt near the lively marketplace or by a quiet stream where she could have communed with God? Yes, and couldn't they have missed the coming Child? God's serendipities do come in odd places, but most often within the household of God.

Here again one may reflect on the prayers of parents, the devotion of the family within the larger family of faith, the blessing of the elders, and their formative impact on the newborn. What powerful forces are at work in blessing children and celebrating their appearing before the Lord!

Once more we cannot fail to see in this lesson the shadow of the cross falling over this blessed event. There is threat as well as promise in the words spoken. The Babe will share real humanity, and what parent has failed to weep a bit for the hurts they know lie ahead for a young babe? More than the average child, this One will give himself as a sacrifice for others. As the sacrificial ritual had required giving life for life, a sacrifice for the new life begun, so Jesus would give himself as the ultimate "life for life" in completing his mission. How could Mary and Joseph fully comprehend this? What lies in store for each blessed child? It sufficed for them to return home and nurture the Child in the context of a faithful home.

St. Matthias, Apostle

FEBRUARY 24

Lutheran	Roman Catholic*	Episcopal
Isa. 66:1–2		Acts 1:15–26
Acts 1:15–26	Acts 1:15–17, 20–26	Phil. 3:13–21
Luke 6:12–16	John 15:9–17	John 15:1, 6–16

EXEGESIS

First Lesson: Isa. 66:1–2. This poem in Third Isaiah turns from discussion of the unfaithful (chap. 65) to that of the faithful and their true worship. The temple is in ruins, and the postexilic fervor for rebuilding the temple and restoring legitimate sacrifice to God presumably gives the theological backdrop for this discourse on that which constitutes true worship. The prophet emphasizes the worship of the heart and life in opposition to externals such as the temple, ceremonials, and even sacrifices (continuing to vv. 3 and 4). The text turns our attention from those externals to the worshiping faithful person.

Just as Yahweh announced to David through the prophet Nathan (cf. 2 Sam. 7), he does not need a house, for indeed all heaven and earth is his dwelling. His throne is in heaven (cf. Ps. 11:4; 103:19, etc.), and his true "footstool" is not the temple but all the earth. Just as Jeremiah and Ezekiel earlier had to challenge the edifice complex in Israel, so Third Isaiah attacks these pious clichés and with a rhetorical question dismisses the notion that Yahweh needs a house or "place of rest" (so the temple is described in Ps. 132:8, 14 and 1 Chron. 28:2).

The affirmation of v. 2 is that all these things, not only house or temple but indeed all creation, already belong to the Creator. Just as it had earlier been folly to believe that God was limited to bricks and mortar and the specific location in Jerusalem at the time of the Exile,

*May 14.

so now it is deemed folly to assume that the chief end of man is to provide for God in this material way. The one to whom God will look in favor or for whom he will have regard (cf. Isa. 63:15) is the person who is humble and contrite in spirit (cf. Isa. 57:15; Pss. 34:18; 51:15–17) and who trembles at his word, or has reverence for his word (cf. Ezra 9:4; 10:3, etc.). The description here and the scathing rejection of sacrifices in vv. 3 and 4 to follow are consistent with the classical prophetic text which attacked the emptiness of the cult when divorced from morality and righteous living (such as Amos 5:21–24; Mic. 6:6–8; Isa. 1:12–17). The Lord will look down with favor upon the humble, contrite, and reverent faithful, and will move to relieve their affliction (cf. Pss. 34:18; 113:5–7).

Much later, Stephen picked up on this text to attack those who clung to the temple and religious institutions while remaining a "stiff-necked" people who resisted God and his Spirit (Acts 7:48–51). The Episcopal First Lesson is Acts 1:15–26, discussed below as the Lutheran Second Lesson.

Second Lesson: Acts 1:15–26. This passage takes up "in those days" between ascension and Pentecost and constitutes the only reference in Scripture to Matthias, the apostle chosen to replace Judas and to fill out the Twelve. Peter, the rock (Matt. 16:18) and one to whom the risen Lord had appeared (Luke 24:34; 1 Cor. 15:5), was characteristically the man of action and initiative. He addressed the assemblage of 120 persons, setting the actions of Judas in scriptural context. It was common in the early church, and indeed in every period until the rise of modern biblical scholarship, to cite detached bits and pieces of the OT to show their fulfillment in Christ or in the early church.

Peter applies portions of the psalms to the actions of Judas in betrayal. Believing that the Spirit spoke through those texts in deeper ways than Israel earlier knew, Peter gives scriptural authority and fulfillment for the happenings. Judas had had a "lot" or portion in their ministry as the Twelve (v. 17). In a parenthetical statement (vv. 18–19) he gives some details of the story—no doubt added for the edification of Theophilus, to whom this book was addressed.

Peter appeals to the psalms (69:25), arguing that the enemies of David are identical with him whose house has now become desolate,

namely the enemy of the new David, Jesus. He further argues
(Ps. 109:8) that the office of this enemy should be taken by another—
that is, they should replace him in the apostolic Twelve. The word
"office" or bishopric, charge, or overseership is the same in sub-
stance as the terms "diaconate" (ministry) or "apostleship" in v. 25.

It is important to note the qualification required of those to be
nominated for this replacement position: they must have had personal
contact with and regular association with Jesus from his baptism to
his ascension. The work to which they are called is that of being a
witness to the resurrection. It is clear that the number twelve, parallel
to the twelve tribes of Israel, was important and to be maintained
(cf. Rev. 21:14). The two men nominated are not well-known and do
not appear elsewhere in Scripture. Eusebius notes that both were
among the seventy (Luke 10:1).

Matthias has been identified with Matthew by some, but there is
little reason to make that connection. There is no clear tradition about
him other than this text. All we know is that he qualified as one who
had gone about with Jesus throughout his earthly ministry and was
deemed by the eleven to be a fit nominee to join them as witnesses.

The method of selection combines the piety of prayer and the OT
practice of casting lots (cf. Lev. 16:8) in order that the Lord may guide
the choice. Some commentators remind us that this happened before
the outpouring of the Spirit at Pentecost—lots were not used after
that. Others note that despite the pious intentions here, God had a
different idea: the selection of Paul as an "untimely" apostle and
witness. It is interesting to note the double meaning of the Greek word
kleros, "lot." It implies the lots cast, a kind of throwing of the dice
(Prov. 16:33) which determines the will of the Lord; but it also may
imply the "lot" or portion (Acts 1:17 or 8:21, for example). We should
observe that this "lot" word is the root of the terms "cleric" or
"clergy," which we affirm to have a share or portion in ministry but
also to have been chosen by God. The one on whom the lot fell was in
fact chosen to have a lot or portion in the apostolic ministry.

The Episcopal Second Lesson is Phil. 3:13–21. This text calls the
disciples to the strenuous race of the Christian life following Paul's
example and warns that there are many enemies of the cross of Christ,
as Judas had been. The final note is one of confidence in the saving
power of Christ to rule and overrule in such threatening matters.

Gospel: Luke 6:12–16. The account of Jesus' appointing the Twelve is found in the other two synoptic Gospels as well (Matt. 10:2–4 and Mark 3:13–19). In John's Gospel Jesus simply affirms that he called the Twelve (John 6:70), and a listing of the Twelve is given in Acts (1:13). It is interesting that the synoptics vary in their listings— both in the order and even in the names (Mark having Thaddaeus, and Matthew having either Thaddaeus or Lebbaeus, in place of Judas son of James). It is clear that the number twelve and designation of the group was of more significance than the individuals, although certainly Peter, James, John, and Andrew head the list.

Our text intends to say that Jesus consciously designated twelve as the symbolic continuation of the twelve tribes. They are to be the heart and core of the new Israel (Luke 22:30), the nucleus of the new people of God. The selection of this group out of the larger company of the disciples (6:17) was not done lightly but only after an agonizing night of prayer.

In this case Jesus went up to "the mountain"—rendered "the hills" in the RSV. Although this mountain is not named, it would appear to carry great symbolic meaning when one thinks of the supreme OT revelation of God on the mountain (Exod. 19), Elijah's encounter with God on the mountain (1 Kings 19:8, 11), the mount of transfiguration (Luke 9:28 and parallels), and the like. Luke's account leads into the discourse on the plain, stressing the movement back down into life in the world with the announcement of the kingdom and of judgment. In Matthew the Sermon on the Mount is followed some time later by the appointing of the Twelve.

V. 12 indicates that this is no routine retreat for prayer; it uses unique terminology for (1) "continuing all night" or "passing the night in watching," which expresses a fervent and earnest wrestling in prayer, and (2) "prayer to God," which expresses a profound communication. The choice of terms tells us that this prayer vigil involved an immediacy of dialogue with God in the selection process.

After the night of prayer, Jesus called to himself the disciples, chose the Twelve, and gave them the name "apostles"—it was God who through Jesus did the calling and the choosing. Their designation expresses "ones sent out." Matthew's Gospel adds more details about the term, indicating that they were sent out as extensions of Jesus' own ministry (Matt. 10:1, 6–8).

Although it is clear that some others in addition to the Twelve listed were accounted "apostles" (Acts 14:14 mentions Barnabas, and Rom. 16:7 two additional ones), nevertheless it appears sure that Jesus selected twelve for special ministry. Although Luke does not spell out the task of the Twelve, this episode moves directly into the healings and teachings on the plain—which ministry of Jesus they were to extend.

Some of the apostles appear frequently in the Gospels, others are heard from no more. We know that they were "eyewitnesses and ministers of the word" (Luke 1:2). Judas would fail and have to be replaced (see Acts 1:15–26). We know that Matthew was a tax collector whom Jesus called (Matt. 9:9; Mark 2:14; and Luke 5:27), that he gave a feast in his house to which other "publicans and sinners" were invited, much to the consternation of the Pharisees (Matt. 9:10; Mark 2:15; and Luke 5:29), and that he had two names, Levi and Matthew, possibly receiving the new name Matthew upon becoming a Christian, even as Simon became Peter. Tradition asserts that Matthew first preached among the Jews, and surely the Gospel bearing his name has that orientation. More about him we do not know. These were ordinary men chosen by an extraordinary One for a task which would "lift up" Jesus (John 12:32) but which would not win for them personal and individual honors and distinction (cf. Luke 22:26 and parallels).

HOMILETICAL INTERPRETATION

First Lesson: Isa. 66:1–2. This text will remind the preacher of the many prophetic assaults on superficial religious practice. It is not with buildings and cultus that the Lord is concerned, but rather with the humble and contrite hearts of believers. One must be careful in handling this theme not to reject all sacred places, religious ceremonials, and institutional forms; however, these must be put in proper perspective. The church needs to hear again the call to be "sent out" ones, whose proper service is in the world in response to the Lord. Retreating to the sanctuary is important for spiritual rest, refreshment, and renewing of the apostolic charge, but the "worship service" should always be only prelude to worship by service.

Just as this prophecy of Isaiah was unsettling to Zerubbabel and his followers who strove so hard to rebuild the temple, so the preaching of service and of benevolent giving may run in stiff competition with those laboring to pay off building debts, developing organ funds, and generally tending to the institutional machinery. God's favor is not bought by giving (even tithing!) and church attendance but rather is gained by responsive reverence ("trembling") for his word which issues in responsive lives combining faith and action.

Second Lesson: Acts 1:15–26. The full complement of twelve is necessary for the new Israel to be prepared for the new tasks after Pentecost. One is struck with the relative obscurity of many of this chosen number. For many of them, their deeds were not recorded and no personal glory and honor came to them. Here the pastor may celebrate the achievements and dedication of countless generations of God's unsung heroes. There have been genuine heroes of the faith from the early church to today, but the church would not have spread or endured without God's little people. In our own church and community we may celebrate today "the Matthias people" who have known the risen Lord, regularly associated with him in their devotion, and gone out as ones sent to witness to the resurrection in quiet, loving deeds of compassion and service.

The Philippians text reminds us that our calling is not to a place of ease (temple or sanctuary) but to the race of faith. In that running the pastor may call his flock to a relinquishing of both good and bad in the past. People may be freed from the burden of "being somebody," even in the Lord's service, and may be challenged to see each day as a new beginning. The reminder that enemies and betrayers abound may be linked with the psalm for the day (Ps. 56), which is a fervent prayer for deliverance from enemies and an affirmation of trust in the saving God who goes with his sent ones.

Gospel: Luke 6:12–16. Just as the casting of lots in Acts was an attempt to let the Lord do the replacement choosing, so in Luke it is clear that Jesus wrestles with the initial selection in a prayer vigil, seeking that the Lord's will be done. The preacher may wish to underscore how much more necessary it is for us to be fervent in prayer when selecting officers, choosing committees, and designating speakers and witnesses. This may be the point for discussion of the spiritual qualifications and preparation of those who are our church leaders. Before they take up their representative tasks, they should be known as persons of "humble and contrite heart," persons who have been for some time in the company of the faithful both coming in to worship and going out to serve, persons who "tremble at his word" and who know themselves to be called not to a rocking chair but to the race of faith. In our practices of selection there will be no throwing of the lot, no direct designation of leaders by Jesus, but whatever the selection process, let the preacher reaffirm that it be done in the context of prayer and the openness to God's choosing: it is our lot to share in the extension of Jesus' ministry as ones sent out.

The Annunciation of Our Lord

MARCH 25

Lutheran	Roman Catholic	Episcopal
Isa. 7:10–14; 8:10c	Isa. 7:10–14	Isa. 7:10–14
1 Tim. 3:16	Heb. 10:4–10	Heb. 10:5–10
Luke 1:26–38	Luke 1:26–38	Luke 1:26–38

EXEGESIS

First Lesson: Isa. 7:10–14; 8:10c. This passage follows hard upon the encounter between King Ahaz and the prophet Isaiah in the Fuller's Field where the king inspected the defenses and reservoir of water. There Isaiah staunchly appealed to Ahaz to stand firm in his faith in God and to resist the pressure of the Syro-Ephraimite alliance against his kingdom Judah in 734 B.C. The prophet's son Shearjashub ("a remnant shall return") stood with the prophet as a sign of judgment on Ahaz for his intention to resist this alliance and capitulate to Assyria rather than standing firm in faith in Yahweh.

In our passage the prophet approaches the king once again. As spokesman for the Lord, Isaiah challenges Ahaz to seek a sign from the Lord in this matter. However, Ahaz responds piously that he "will not put the Lord to the test" (cf. Deut. 6:16). That one may faithfully seek such a sign is clear in the case of Gideon (Judg. 6:16–17). At issue here is the fact that Ahaz has made his own judgment and is unwilling to risk a more clear word from the Lord than the prophet has already delivered, namely one which would refute his plans. Isaiah intentionally contrasts their faith commitments when he speaks to Ahaz of *your* God (v. 11) and of *my* God who is displeased (v. 13).

The crux of the matter comes in v. 14 where the prophet insists that God will give a sign whether it is sought or not, and in the giving there is both threat and promise. A "sign" was a testimony, something that gave assurance to one who beheld it (Exod. 3:12; Josh. 2:12; 1 Sam. 10:7, 9, etc.). The sign had very contemporary relevance to human faith and actions.

The nature of the sign in v. 14 for King Ahaz is clear: a young woman will bear a child, and before the child reaches the age of moral discernment the Syro-Ephraimite threat will have disappeared and the devastating intrusion of Assyria will have reduced those who endure to a nomadic state (so vv. 15–25 clearly show). There is no indication that the force of the sign is in a miraculous birth or in the naming of the child; it is rather in the historical situation Judah is about to confront because of the faithless political decisions of Ahaz.

The debate of the centuries for Christian interpreters has raged about the term "the young woman" and about the name Immanuel. In the Hebrew the "young woman" is a girl of marriageable age, and the technical term for "a virgin" is not employed. The Septuagint, a Greek version, does use the term "virgin," and of course this is the term picked up by Matthew (1:22–23) for application seven hundred years later to the birth of Jesus. Projecting the "sign" centuries into the future takes all force out of it for Ahaz. Whatever it means later in the wisdom of God, it had specific and more limited meaning for King Ahaz and was likely spoken about some young woman present to the discussion.

The name Immanuel, meaning "God with us," appears also in Isa. 8:8, 10c as an affirmation of trust and confidence in God even in the crisis of judgment. Just as the naming of Isaiah's son "a remnant shall return" expressed both threat and promise, so "God with us" expresses the notion that the righteous God will have his day of judging but will ultimately save. For "the young woman" so to name her child and for such historical events to come to pass so soon would indeed be a "sign" to Ahaz that God is king and the lord of history. The deeper meaning of the prophet's words has been revealed only by the passing of the centuries and the further intervention of God.

Second Lesson: 1 Tim. 3:16. The author quotés an early Christian hymn to climax the first half of his epistle. From chap. 4 onward he will give a variety of exhortations related to putting the faith into practice. One clear emphasis will be upon the resisting of heresy ("godless and silly myths" in 4:7, for example). He has said that it is necessary to have order and proper conduct in the church and that the church must stand as a bulwark of truth (3:15). He underscores that "truth" by quoting what must have been a familiar hymn. The hymnic form is clear in the six lines, each beginning with a verb and followed by prepositional phrases. Unfortunately, we have only this fragment and the full interpretation is difficult.

The author's introduction may be viewed as a Christian counterpart to the Ephesian cry "Great is Artemis of the Ephesians!" (Acts 19:28). He solemnly declares, "Great indeed is the mystery of our religion!" He notes that "we confess" this, and a good translation would be "beyond all question" or "undoubtedly." He affirms that our faith is beyond dispute. The "mystery" refers to the hidden work of God now revealed to those who have the eyes of faith (1 Cor. 2:6–8). Mystery religions abounded in that day, and the author here affirms that what they sought to discover had in fact been revealed in the coming of Christ in the flesh.

In the Greek the quote begins with "who," and this clearly has reference to Christ, as the poem indicates. Some variant texts read "God" and others "which," neither of which variants should be accepted. For clarity of interpretation, the RSV correctly reads "he."

"Was manifested in the flesh" emphasizes the true humanity of Jesus. His epiphany was in the weakness and humility of human flesh (cf. Heb. 2:14–18; Phil. 2:7).

"Vindicated in the Spirit" gives the spiritual foil to the above; that is, he was truly God. "Vindicated" or "declared righteous" means that Jesus was shown in fact to be the righteous Son of God in his spiritual nature. The contrast of the two natures is seen in other epistles (Rom. 1:3–4 and 1 Pet. 3:18) in such a way as to suggest that the resurrection may be implied in our simple text.

"Seen by angels" is best understood not in terms of the angels encountered in his earthly ministry (wilderness temptation, transfiguration, empty tomb) but in terms of his being worshiped by all men and angels (cf. 1 Pet. 3:22; Eph. 3:10; Heb. 1:6).

"Preached among the nations" expresses the missionary work of the church in all the world, perhaps having emphasis on the movement to the Gentiles. As the Christ is worshiped above (angels), so he is proclaimed below (to mankind).

"Believed on in the world" expresses the response of faith in the world, or perhaps even in the whole cosmos.

"Taken up in glory" seems out of sequence. The hymn was probably attempting to give not a historical account but a theological affirmation moving from human to divine, earthly to heavenly— implications of the manifestation of God in the flesh. This allusion to the ascension may be viewed in the hymn as referring to the ultimate consummation of Christ's universal reign.

The Roman Catholic Second Lesson for the day is Heb. 10:4–10 (Episcopal, 10:5–10), which centers on the application of Ps. 40:6–8. This text focuses on the obedience of Christ and the way in which his sacrifice does away with the old sacrificial system. The sacrifice of the new covenant is obedience, and Christ's fulfillment of the psalm, read in Hebrews as "Lo, I have come to do thy will, O God," may be considered with Mary's obedient and faithful yielding to the annunciation where she says, "Let it be to me according to your word" (Luke 1:38).

Gospel: Luke 1:26–38. The psalm for this day is a royal psalm (45) and gives exalted praise to the king. Of particular note is the stress on the one from the house of David whose throne will be forever. It is the birth of the One who fulfills this that is announced in our passage.

Some attention must be given to Luke 1:5–25. Luke gives the account of the angel Gabriel's announcement of the birth of John the

Baptist. Our passage is clearly patterned on that one and intends to show the superiority of Mary in her response and the superiority of Jesus in his person and work.

The events are tied together in v. 26 "in the sixth month" of Elizabeth's pregnancy. Once more it is the angel Gabriel, now appearing in Nazareth of Galilee. The move to the obscure outer fringes of the world fulfills the prophecy of Isaiah (9:1–2). Although this is the only text affirming the virgin birth (it is not a part of the apostolic preaching, nor is it assumed elsewhere in the Gospels, save in the parenthetical note in Luke's genealogy in 3:23), it is clear that the word "virgin" is employed (cf. discussion of Isa. 7 above). That Mary was betrothed to Joseph would seem to undercut any notion that Mary intended to be a virgin perpetually. That so many NT epistles indicate that a major heretical threat was that of judging Jesus to be fully God and of denying his humanity (the Docetic heresy) would imply that this virgin birth was early in the tradition and well-known. It is Joseph who is designated as of the house of David, and it is by that natural parental relationship that it is clear that Jesus is legally, at least, of the house of David, although it is widely assumed that Mary was also of the house of David—perhaps implied in v. 32. Jesus' being of the house of David as opposed to John's parents' being of the house of Aaron is one more evidence here of the superiority of Jesus. Although no interpretation of Mary's name is given, it has the same root as Miriam's (cf. the latter's song of victory in Exod. 15:21).

Gabriel appeared and spoke rather bluntly to Zechariah, but here he uses a deferential greeting: "Hail, O favored one" (v. 28). God has shown favor or grace to Mary, who is the recipient of grace, but in no way does the text imply that she is a source of grace in herself. "The Lord is with you" is a conscious parallel to and variation of the Immanuel theme (Isa. 7:14). Mary is not troubled by the sight of the angel as was Zechariah, but wonders at what he says. As with Zechariah, the angel attempts to calm her fears, and announces the coming birth of a child to be named Jesus. Luke does not expound upon the meaning of the name, but Matthew does indicate the meaning "salvation of Yahweh" (Matt. 1:21). It was a relatively common name, Jesus or Joshua, but here had an uncommonly significant relationship to his person and work.

Vv. 32–33 clearly recall Isaiah's messianic words (Isa. 9:6–7), indicating that the promises to David (cf. 2 Sam. 7:14; Pss. 2:7; 45:6; 89:26–27, etc.) are fulfilled in Jesus. This One from the house of David will rule forever and will be Son to the Father in a unique, saving relationship.

Mary marvels not at the content of the promised fulfillment but at the mode of its accomplishment. As a betrothed, virginal woman she had no husband. Gabriel announces that the birth will be a new creative act of the Holy Spirit (v. 35), who would overshadow her and bring forth the Second Adam, thus bringing about a new creation. Shadows of the OT fall on our text: just as the cloud covered the tent of meeting and filled it with the glory of God, so the Spirit would cover Mary and fill her with the glory of God's Son. One should note the cloud covering at the mount of transfiguration and the cloud covering at the ascension. This strong symbolic language signifies that this is God's doing; this will be a holy Child, Son of the Holy God.

As a sign reinforcing the announcement, Mary is told that her kinswoman Elizabeth will bear a son in her old age, overcoming her barrenness. As it was not impossible for God to overcome that problem (cf. Sarah's child in her old age in Gen. 18:14), so Mary's conception is not too hard for God either.

Mary does not laugh at the prospect or doubt it but rather yields to the calling of God in model piety. She submits, saying she is the "handmaid" of the Lord (cf. 1 Sam. 1:11 of Hannah). The word has even a more forceful meaning as "slave" or "servant." As David had oftentimes been termed "servant of the Lord" in the psalms (78:70; 89:3, etc.), so now Mary takes the servant role in obedience with nothing held back.

HOMILETICAL INTERPRETATION

First Lesson: Isa. 7:10–14; 8:10c. This text raises for the preacher questions of faith and history, theology and politics. What bearing does one's faith in God as the Lord of history have on real-life decisions of a military/political nature in a threatening world? Is it naive to call for trust in God when tanks are rolling and warplanes take flight? Yet the coin of our realm affirms, "In God we trust."

Such times are times of our temptation. We would have God pass a miracle that would compel belief (for such reasons many emphasize miraculous virgin birth), or with Ahaz we suggest that we will ask no "sign" from God in such national and international affairs but rather make our own decisions and preparations for defense. The preacher may grapple with the implications of the fully revealed "sign" in Christ, "God with us." "If God is for us, who is against us?" Paul wrote (Rom. 8:31).

As the text relates specifically to the annunciation, we are a full nine months away from the fulfilling birth. Can we trust in our day that God has not abandoned us and that the birth of this Child of God has anything to say in our history? Such trust was too much for Ahaz, who of course did not have the revelation of Christ as we do. Even so, are we more trusting?

Second Lesson: 1 Tim. 3:16. God's ways are mysterious to us. His saving intention was revealed not in might but in humility. The epiphany song in 1 Timothy celebrates the mixture of the human and the divine in Christ. His person and life constitute a powerful sign of the intervention of God, the heart of what we preach to the whole world. Do we ponder what we affirm so glibly in creeds or what we sing in our hymnody? We may ask whether such affirmations are appropriate only in the sanctuary where one may speak of angels and mysteries, or whether they are also "believed on in the world" as our text states.

The Hebrews passage centers on obedience as the appropriate sacrifice of the new covenant. Here we reflect on the impact of "God with us" on our life-styles. Can we respond to his obedience with the humility and trust that Mary showed at the annunciation? What is our obedience in God's new creation?

Gospel: Luke 1:26–38. Today's festival centers in this text. The shocking announcement is that the age-old expectations are fulfilled in Christ, that God has broken into our history. From our side of the life and death of Jesus we can look back with Paul and say God was at work here, for indeed "God was in Christ reconciling the world to himself" (2 Cor. 5:19).

The proclamation may focus on the response of Mary to this announcement. Protestants in particular are cautious about praising Mary's model piety lest we mistakenly suggest that she was sinless, perfect in all ways, perhaps even divine. In that caution let us not fail to see the beauty and power of her yielding to the Lord as his servant. As God was "in Christ," as Jesus was formed in Mary, cannot we yield to the Spirit's invasion into frail humanity and see that he can bring to birth God's saving power and action even in the likes of us? What fruit we will bear will be not of our doing but of God. He wills to abide in us and work through us (cf. John 15). Let the preacher wrestle with that announcement for the Marys and Josephs, and Bettys and Carls, in our day. The incarnation begun by the Spirit in a humble and trusting young woman, and continued by the Spirit in the obedience of a carpenter's Son who fulfilled all messianic hopes, continues now in the responsive obedience of generations of simple folk who extend that incarnation in the world (John 17:11, 18). We celebrate the beginning of that incarnation. We properly respond when we yield to its continuing.

St. Mark, Evangelist

APRIL 25

Lutheran	Roman Catholic	Episcopal
Isa. 52:7–10		Isa. 52:7–10
2 Tim. 4:6–11, 18	1 Pet. 5:5b–14	Eph. 4:7–8, 11–16
Mark 1:1–15	Mark 16:15–20	Mark 1:1–15 or Mark 16:15–20

EXEGESIS

The Second Lesson and Gospel for this day occasion some problems in light of contemporary biblical scholarship. The selection of texts implies the traditional connection of all NT references to someone named Mark with the John Mark mentioned in Acts (12; 13; and 15), and that this Mark is the author of the Gospel of Mark. It is by no means certain that the Mark referred to in 1 Pet. 5:13 and in 2 Tim. 4:11 (or for that matter the Mark in Col. 4:10 and Philem. 24) is the same individual. There is no evidence other than tradition that these texts refer to Mark the evangelist. There is general agreement that the

2 Timothy text is not Pauline, but its writer does intend to present Paul's last days and likely does refer to the John Mark of Acts. Although little can be said about Mark the evangelist in a definitive way, we have attempted to deal with the lectionary texts with sensitivity to both traditional and critical interpretations.*

First Lesson: Isa. 52:7–10. In this lyrical outbursting of joy, the poet/prophet sees the fulfillment of his message of comfort (Isa. 40). The text draws up the themes of Deutero-Isaiah and speaks to the faithful yearnings of the psalmist who steadily cried for the Lord to deliver, to show mercy, to assert himself, and to become exalted (Ps. 57).

In Isa. 52:1–6 this climax is anticipated. Now the prophet uses an adaptation of the hymn-of-praise form to summon the people to rejoice on the basis of a series of eschatological perfect verbs expressing the action of God. Having languished in exile and dwelt in the deep darkness of the ruin of Jerusalem, the people and the city are recalled to light and life in the deliverance from Babylon and the restoration of Jerusalem.

In v. 7 the herald, or "evangelist," comes on the mountains. The cry "how beautiful" expresses the timely and welcome coming of such a messenger (cf. Nah. 1:15). "Feet" stands for the messenger, the part for the whole. Paul uses this terminology for the Christian evangelists (Rom. 10:15). The message is threefold: peace, good, and salvation. The herald proclaims God's victory in the release and that now at last "all is well." The summation spoken to Zion is that "God reigns," picking up on the strong theme that Yahweh is king and fulfilling Nathan's promise to David of an everlasting kingship in Zion, now with God himself as King rather than one from the house of David (cf. 2 Sam. 7).

V. 8 carries the fulfillment further. The watchmen are not the prophets of old (such as Habakkuk) but those who look from the ruined walls of Jerusalem for some sign of hope, of the return of Yahweh's presence and favor. Upon seeing and hearing the mes-

---

*For a concise discussion of the difficulties in identifying the author of the Gospel of Mark and in making connections between the various references to someone named Mark in the NT, we refer the reader to Paul J. Achtemeier's *Mark* in the Proclamation Commentaries series (Philadelphia: Fortress Press, 1975), pp. 111–14.

senger on the hills, they break into song. The seeing "eye to eye"
expresses the clear and immediate vision of what God has done
(cf. Num. 14:14). What is perceived is that Ezekiel's vision of the
return of the "glory" of Yahweh to Zion has been completed—the
perfect tense of certainty (cf. Ezek. 43:1–5).

With the exuberance of Hebrew poetry, even the inanimate ruins
of Jerusalem are summoned into song at this word of deliverance.
Who can fail to think of the breathing of new life into the dry bones
(Ezek. 37)?

The final verse (10) indicates that Yahweh the warrior has thrown
back the cloak and readied himself for action. The arm is not held to
the bosom (Ps. 74:11) but readied for battle (cf. Isa. 40:10; 51:9; 53:1,
etc.). This saving action is not for the nation only but is to be seen
universally. All the nations will see the deliverance from Babylon and
the merciful returning and restoration of Jerusalem. The kingship of
God seen in his mighty acts is announced and celebrated.

Second Lesson: 2 Tim. 4:6–11, 18. Here the author becomes a
bearer of the Pauline tradition and assumes the role of Paul nearing
the end of his ministry and concerned with those who will carry on the
work. In v. 6 the expression in the Greek is quite emphatic, "As for
me," set in contrast with the charge to Timothy (v. 5, "As for you")
to keep on working and to fulfill his ministry. "As for me," the author
in the role of Paul writes, "I am at the point of being sacrificed." The
verb expresses the pouring out of a drink offering (cf. Phil. 2:17). He
notes that his time of departure is at hand. The term for departure is
"unloosening," used either of dismantling a tent or unloosening the
ropes of a ship about to set sail. One may connect the notion of the
drink offering with the practice of making such an offering before a
ship sets sail. At any rate, it is clear that the author is speaking of
Paul's final departure, his death, about which Paul spoke earlier using
the same verb (Phil. 1:23).

The author continues the discussion of the end of Paul's ministry by
using two sporting images: the fight and the race. First, he has fought
the good fight—one for noble ends (cf. 1 Tim. 6:12). Second, he has
finished the race—one that he had steadfastly and with singleness of
mind been running (Phil. 3:13–14; Acts 20:24) and about which his
only concern was that he should not run in vain (Phil. 2:16). As he had

instructed Timothy to keep the faith and keep in the race (and no doubt had instructed others, including Mark), the author indicates that Paul has kept the faith—either he has kept the Christian faith entrusted to him (1 Tim. 6:20; 2 Tim. 1:12, 14), or he has kept his pledge and followed the rules of the race of life (2 Tim. 2:5).

The reward that the author sees in store for Paul is the crown of righteousness—not the distant object of obtaining righteousness, for that has already been given by Christ, but more likely the reward or crown given in the race of righteousness just as there was a crown for racing, a crown for fighting, and the like (the genitive being one of particular interests). The author in Paul's role does not fear the coming of the Righteous Judge, knowing Paul has kept the faith and on that Day he and indeed all who love the Lord's appearing (cf. waiting for Christ in Phil. 3:20) will be so rewarded. One should remember the OT concept of that Day. It was the Day of the Lord for which many yearned and expectantly waited. The prophets often warned that the sinful people would be surprised and dismayed when it came, for the righteous judge would bring painful judgment (cf. Amos 5:18–20). Here the author confidently anticipates that Day for Paul, who has been made righteous in Christ.

The text now turns to more personal concerns in the author's presentation of Paul's last days. He appeals to Timothy to come to him quickly before he passes on. He notes that Demas, who had formerly been imprisoned with him (Col. 4:14), has forsaken him due to his love of this present world as opposed to the kingdom of God (cf. 1 Tim. 6:17; Titus 2:12). Others listed have gone elsewhere in Christian mission. Only Luke remains among his close associates.

The author in Paul's role asks Timothy to "pick up" Mark on the way to him—implying that Mark was engaged in ministry somewhere on the route between them. Mark had shared in mission with Paul and Barnabas (Acts 12:25) but had turned back to Jerusalem (Acts 13:13). When Barnabas later had wanted Mark to accompany them again, Paul refused and there was a sharp and painful break between them (Acts 15:36–39). Following the traditional identification of Mark, it appears that these differences had long ago been healed and Paul had shared other imprisonments and mission work with Mark (Col. 4:10; Philem. 24). The traditional view suggests that Mark reached Rome and was spoken of by Peter as "my son," probably implying that Peter had brought Mark to the faith (1 Pet. 5:13). Here the author in the role of Paul indicates that Mark will be personally useful in serving him (v. 11). This "serving" is the ministry word, *diakonian*, and may imply not only serving Paul but also engaging in ministry with him.

Finally, the writer, on behalf of Paul, expresses faith in God who has preserved him so far and who he believes will rescue him from evil. This is an affirmation not that he will be freed or spared, for he cared little for his life (cf. Phil. 1:21), but that he will be saved from failing or breaking under the pressure. The Lord will bring him to his heavenly kingdom and for that the author gives an outburst of glory to God.

The Episcopal Second Lesson for the day (Eph. 4:7-8, 11-16) speaks of the gifts given to the disciples for the building up of the body of Christ in the unity the members share. When the Ephesians passage speaks of growing in faith and into mature manhood (4:13) and not being children tossed to and fro by every wind of doctrine (4:14), this may involve some reference to Paul's view of Mark's behavior in leaving him earlier. Surely in the end Paul respected Mark as one who had so matured and whose companionship was desired for the up-building of the body and for his own personal comfort.

The Roman Catholic Second Lesson (1 Pet. 5:5b-14) calls for endurance in the face of suffering and ends with greetings from Peter's companions, including "my son Mark" (5:13). As noted above, Peter probably received Mark as a convert into the faith. Tradition has it that Mark was particularly close to Peter, serving as his interpreter (so says Papias of Hierapolis).

Gospel: Mark 1:1-15. Mark was a relatively obscure disciple, who was called, was tested in his ministry (note especially his break and then reconciliation with Paul), matured in the work, and proclaimed the "good news." That proclamation we still hear today in the Gospel that bears his name.

Mark's Gospel is the shortest of the four and moves with vivid, powerful, terse statements loaded with theological impact and with scriptural allusions. These verses move rapidly through the generations of expectant longing for the messiah, the coming of the forerun-

ner, the appearance of Jesus who is the Christ (or Messiah), the
temptation of Jesus, and the summary of the good news which Jesus
both announced as Messenger and embodied as Savior.

The "beginning" for Mark was that of the message of good news,
the term "gospel" not being used in the NT for a written document.
After the title verse (1), Mark refers to "the prophets" (not only
Isaiah but also Malachi), citing the coming of one to prepare the way
for God's new saving action (Isa. 40:3) and specifically words about
the forerunner (Mal. 3:1). Wasting no words or "editorial glue,"
Mark follows the quote with the simple affirmation "John the baptizer
appeared." Let the reader make the deduction that this is fulfillment.
John preached a baptism of repentance, which repentance would
bring forgiveness (cf. Ezek. 36:25). While not "all" from Judea
and Jerusalem may have come, great throngs did come confessing
their sins.

The brief description of John's life-style (v. 6) clearly connects him
with the work of Elijah before (2 Kings 1:8 and Zech. 13:4). John ate
the simple foods the wilderness provided (cf. Lev. 11:22; Deut.
32:13–14). With no further comment Mark moves to the meaning of
the preaching and baptizing ministry of John: it is the work of preparation for the One to come. John contrasts his water baptism with the
baptism of the Holy Spirit that Jesus will bring (cf. Acts 1:5; 11:16).

Again with no interpretive comment, Mark simply announces that
in those days Jesus came from his obscure village in Galilee and was
baptized. Let the reader deduce that this is fulfillment. In this fulfilling
of all righteousness, the sinless one humbled himself, taking the form
of a servant (cf. Phil. 2:6–7). Upon being baptized Jesus saw the Holy
Spirit in the form of a dove. Just as Noah had sent forth a dove to
brood over the waters seeking the land of a new beginning for humankind (Gen. 8:12), so the dove broods over Jesus in whom a new
beginning of the kingdom comes forth.

The words which Jesus heard combine recollections of the royal
theology—the exaltation of the king as son of God (Ps. 2:7)—with the
theology of the servant, the one who would suffer in humble obedience (Isa. 42:1). In this terse statement are combined two major
themes of OT expectation, themes which were most difficult for the
disciples to join until after the resurrection appearances.

There is no simple and beautiful nativity story here; instead we meet the mature Jesus embarking on a painful saving mission. With no transitional discussion, Mark simply says the Spirit drove (a harsh word) Jesus into the wilderness for forty days (parallel to the forty years Israel was in the wilderness) for temptation and battle with Satan. Mark does not give the nature of that tempting as Luke and Matthew do, but it was the same: a challenge to doubt his mission and to take shortcuts to establish the kingdom. In this period of confrontation, loneliness, and threat, God was supporting Jesus by his angels. (Cf. Ps. 91:11–13, where the angels minister and wild animals do not harm. Note also the Test. Naphtali, which indicates that the devil will flee, that the wild beasts will be in fear, and that angels will come.)

Again Mark gives a terse abbreviation of intervening events. John's work of preparation ran its course and he was imprisoned (v. 14), then Jesus came preaching. The Spartan summary of Jesus' message includes the announcement common to the apostolic preaching: that the time was fulfilled, was ripe; that the kingdom of God was at hand; and that the hearers should respond to the events of that kingdom coming in Christ by repentance and by belief in the good news of Jesus. "To repent" was far more than merely to feel sorry and to confess sin. It was rather to turn about, to make a radical change. It can be clearly seen in the path of the Israelites who after the Exodus took a route that would avoid war "lest they repent" and return to Egypt (Exod. 13:17). As the hearers were called to repent and believe, those called by Jesus in the ensuing verses of chap. 1 were to leave their past place and tasks and to follow the Christ.

The Roman Catholic Gospel is a portion of the difficult "addition" to Mark's Gospel (Mark 16:15–20). Here Jesus sends out the apostles to preach and baptize in all the world, to do marvelous signs and the like. It ends with the risen and glorified Lord "working with them" in their preaching and confirming their mission with signs.

HOMILETICAL INTERPRETATION

First Lesson: Isa. 52:7–10. Paul applied this text to the Christian heralds of the gospel (Rom. 10:15). On this day we think of its application to Mark and his witness to the comfort and redemption wrought in Jesus. The victory of God in the OT bringing release of the captives from Babylon and restoration of Jerusalem was but a foretaste of that greater redemption heralded by Mark in his Gospel.

Exposition of this text might lead to reflection on those who faithfully wait and watch for the culmination of God's saving activity. At a time of practical atheism when so many expect so little of God, such a mood of faithful expectancy is sorely needed. When so many messengers of the media bombard us with the bad news, when the institutional church is out of favor and its walls cracked if not shattered, where are the hopeful and expectant ones?

Second Lesson: 2 Tim. 4:6–11, 18. As the author depicts Paul nearing his death, he reflects on the race of faith and exhorts others, like Mark, to persevere in tough times. The writer climaxes this discussion with a doxology in praise of God who has sustained him and is his comfort to the end.

It is touching that the author reaches out for companionship in his last days. One may identify with the common human need to be surrounded by one's friends at the end no matter how firm one's faith may be. The writer has no fears of the Day of the Lord and no fears of dying in the Lord but yearns to complete his days with dear friends like Luke and Timothy and Mark. In his asking for Mark we see how reconciliation between the two has been fully effected. The Ephesians text may be applied to Mark's youthful falling away from Paul and his subsequent maturing in faith to be a stalwart witness. Just so the faithful elderly person may look with joy to the next generation's maturing in the faith and taking up the work of Christ. Just so that elderly witness, who now is confined or limited in his or her ability to be about the work of the church as in earlier years, needs to have the visits and the companionship of those who not only advance the gospel in the world but also take time to visit and comfort their predecessors.

The 1 Peter text may suggest that Mark was a friend and close companion not only of Paul but also of Peter. What greater tribute and blessing could there be than to be summoned by a Paul in his hour of need or to be called by a Peter "my son"?

Gospel: Mark 1:1–15. With the terse and powerful style typical of his Gospel, Mark gives in capsule the heart of the gospel he and the early church preached. The rest of his sixteen chapters will expand on this basic gospel: the promises are fulfilled, the Christ has come announcing and bringing in the kingdom, repent and believe.

Mark himself had responded to that proclamation and fulfillment. He had been tempted in his youth and had held on, to mature in the faith. He had known reconciliation with Paul and more importantly with God through Christ. He then became a powerful witness whose words still call us to repentance and to faith. We know little, really, about Mark, but let us thank God that we know much about Jesus due to Mark's witness in life and writing. Here again is testimony that God uses his little ones for great things.

The Mark 16 text reminds us of the wonders that witnesses like Mark would do and that in the proclamation God continues to work with his disciples. Perhaps we need to be reminded that we do not witness or serve in our own power but in the Lord's. Perhaps the modern Mark needs to hear again, "Lo, I am with you always, to the close of the age" (Matt. 28:20). Mark did not work or write alone; neither do we.

St. Philip and St. James, Apostles

MAY 1

Lutheran	Roman Catholic*	Episcopal
Isa. 30:18–21		Isa. 30:18–21
2 Cor. 4:1–6	1 Cor. 15:1–8	2 Cor. 4:1–6
John 14:8–14	John 14:6–14	John 14:6–14

EXEGESIS

First Lesson: Isa. 30:18–21. There is a fervent plea for the fulfillment of this prophecy of salvation in the psalm reading for today, Ps. 44:1–3, 20–26. In that psalm there is the recollection of God's past

*May 3.

saving actions and the plea for him to tarry no longer in showing mercy (cf. Ps. 77:9; 102:13; 123:2, etc.). Isaiah said earlier, "I will wait for the Lord, who is hiding his face from the house of Jacob, and I will hope in him" (8:17). Here the prophet expresses the patience and gracefulness of God despite Israel's lack of trust documented in prior verses of this chapter.

The connecting link "therefore" either harks back to the positive faith posture (30:15) which the people had rejected or should perhaps be read as a new word introducing the new oracle, as "behold" or "even" or "nevertheless." The thought is clear: as Judah has waited more or less patiently for divine intervention, so God waits for the moment, the ripeness of time for his action on their behalf in grace and mercy. That saving time is imminent, and the prophet declares that God is stirring himself, rising up. He "exalts himself" in his readiness to act.

Isaiah comforts the people, indicating that God has heard their cry and will deliver, just as earlier he had heard the cry of those in bondage in Egypt and moved to save them. Though they may have to endure some continuing hard times symbolized in the food of imprisonment, bread and water, God is about to deliver. Some commentators speculate that the provision of bread and water is a part of the gracious action of God, insuring that their needs are provided for (cf. Isa. 33:16); however, there is no textual support for deleting "of adversity" and "of affliction" here. Instead, we should see that Isaiah expresses hope for deliverance, even though at the time the people must endure deprivations.

A further controversy rages about v. 20 in the interpretation of "the teacher." At issue is the fact that the verb "be hidden" or "hide themselves" is in the plural whereas the noun "teacher" is singular. The RSV takes the singular and interprets this as the Teacher, namely God. This is difficult in that the verse indicates that you will see your Teacher, an unthinkable notion in Israel, where one surely does not see God face-to-face (cf. Exod. 33:20, etc.). One may overcome this difficulty by interpreting the passage to mean that one will once again see the works of God. The alternative is to read the term as "teachers" and to interpret it as speaking of the eschatological teachers or prophets who have had to go into hiding and whose words of comfort with regard to the future have not been heeded. In this approach, which we adopt, the prophet says that once again the teachers will be heard and heeded.

The final verse expresses the new allegiance to the directing words of God—through his teachers. In the saving time about to come, the people will be guided by the fatherly, coaxing voice which will keep them on the right path (cf. the holding by the hand and guiding counsel celebrated in Ps. 73:21–24), saying, "This is the way."

Second Lesson: 2 Cor. 4:1–6. Some reflection on Paul's discussion of the ministry of the new covenant (2 Cor. 3:6ff.) provides a significant backdrop for our text. Paul moves from that discussion of the limited and fading light in the face of Moses and the veil over the old covenant (Exod. 34) to the enduring light in the face of Christ betokening the new creation (cf. Gen. 1). Here he speaks not only of his own ministry but also of that of all the apostles, defending himself (and by implication the others) from charges made against him and perhaps against practices of pagans about them. What he says applies equally to Philip and James, to the apostolic message and its reception. Paul replies to charges of self-seeking and insincerity (cf. 1:17; 2:17, etc.) and has already indicated that their only sufficiency is in Christ, not themselves (3:5).

This ministry of the new covenant which they share has been given by the mercy of God (cf. 1 Cor. 7:25; 15:9–10; 1 Tim. 1:13, 16). In that confidence and God-given sufficiency they do not lose heart, grow lax, or become faint. Rather they speak with boldness (2 Cor. 3:12). From the time of conversion and as an abiding principle, followers of Christ renounce underhanded ways and cunning practices common to Satan and his followers (2 Cor. 11:3, 12–15), that is, the heretics Paul so severely condemns in 2 Corinthians 11. Rather, we apostles, Paul writes, do not tamper with the word of God, meaning both OT Scripture and primarily the word of Jesus, as do those peddlers of the word who seek their own acclaim (cf. 2:17).

The way of the true disciple is to seek the light (John 3:20–21) and to speak plainly the open truth of God. Referring again to the veil discussed in chap. 3, Paul says if anyone does not perceive the gospel plainly, this is due not to any fault in the gospel or its proclamation but to the veil cast over it by the "god of this world." This is a unique expression but clearly refers to Satan. (Cf. the "prince" or "ruler of this world" in John 12:31.)

Paul describes the gospel as light (cf. John 1:5) which radiates from Christ, reflecting the very image of God (v. 4). Whereas the light of the former revelation to Moses was fading (3:7), the light of Christ shines forth as a new creation (paraphrasing Gen. 1:3 in v. 6). As the blinding light shone on Paul at the time of his conversion (Acts 9:3; 22:6; 26:13), so the light shines in the hearts of the believers to give knowledge of the glory of God in the face of Christ, the truth of the divine revelation made fully in Jesus.

What we preach then, Paul says, is not ourselves or for our own glory. Some might feel, and apparently some laid the charge to Paul, that appealing to followers to imitate him (1 Cor. 4:16; 7:7; 11:1) might justify such an accusation of self-seeking. No, we preach only Christ crucified (1 Cor. 2:2) and ourselves as your servants (1 Cor. 3:5; 4:1; 9:19). Here Paul speaks of the apostolic ministry as one of humility like that of Jesus, who emptied himself (Phil. 2:7) and who said that he "came not to be served but to serve" (Mark 10:45). In this defense of his ministry Paul defends all apostolic ministry and in effect makes an appeal for all disciples to "have that mind among yourselves, which you have in Christ Jesus" (Phil. 2:5).

The Roman Catholic Second Lesson for the day is 1 Cor. 15:1–8, which speaks of the gospel which Paul had preached and by which salvation comes if we hold fast to it. Paul goes on to recount the heart of the gospel in Jesus' death for our sins, burial, and resurrection. In those resurrection appearances Philip is included among "the Twelve" and James is included by name.

Gospel: John 14:8–14. Today we deal with two apostles: Philip and James. The feast celebrates Philip the Apostle, not the evangelist of Acts 6, and there are a few other texts which refer to him (John 1; 12; 14; and Acts 1) in addition to the apostolic lists. The James in question is "the less" or "younger" (Mark 15:40), the son of Alphaeus—not James son of Zebedee (celebrated on July 25), about whom we know a bit more, nor James the Lord's brother. The mother of this James appears more prominently in the Gospels than he does (cf. Matt. 27:56; Mark 16:1; Luke 24:10), and she may have been sister to Mary the mother of Jesus if we take Clopas to be another name for Alphaeus (John 19:25). The Gospel for the day centers on Philip; however, discussion about Philip and Thomas here may well reflect the attitudes and questions of James and others of the apostles.

Jesus indicated that the disciples did not know the way to the Father's house, which could not be prepared for them unless he went to the Father (John 14:1–4). Thomas responded with a typical questioning attitude, asking how they could know where Jesus was going and the way implied. It is at the point of Jesus' response to Thomas that the Roman Catholic and Episcopal Gospel for the day takes up (v. 6). Jesus connects our lesson with the earlier passage about the way, indicating that he is the way, the truth, and the life and that no one comes to the Father but by him; that is, the owner's son will have to show the way to the place prepared. Jesus goes on to say that Thomas should have known him and his relation to the Father (v. 7) and, in what is partially a rebuke for that lack of vision and even more a promise, adds that from now on they understand and have seen the Father in him.

At this point Philip demonstrates once more his "show me" pragmatic inclination. One may recall his pragmatic invitation to Nathanael to "come and see" (John 1:45–46), his dealing with the practical concerns of the feeding of the multitude (John 6:5–7), and his involvement with Greeks who wished to "see Jesus" (John 12:21). Now Philip, not satisfied with the response given to Thomas and equally full of questions, wishes for himself to "see" the Father. Our psalm for the day (44:1–3, 20–26) is relevant here, as the psalmist cries out to know God today. He writes that we have heard of God by the ear and know his mighty acts in the past (v. 1) but now yearn for him to act in our day and no longer hide his face (v. 24). In concert with the religious quest of the ages, and especially the yearnings of the psalmists (Pss. 42:1–2; 17:15), Philip asks for a theophany like Moses' (Exod. 24:9–11; 33:18) without heeding the dangers in seeing God face-to-face (Exod. 33:20).

Jesus shows some frustration with Philip because Philip had been with him so long (among the first called, in John 1:43) and like the rest of the disciples failed to understand this and many other things (John 10:6; 12:16, etc.). It would only be after the gift of the Spirit that they would really perceive what Jesus had said about himself and the

Father (John 1:18; 12:45). Although they would not directly see God (1 John 4:12, 20), they would come to understand that Jesus reflects the very image of God (2 Cor. 4:4; Col. 1:15; and Heb. 1:3).

If you cannot believe these things I have taught, Jesus said, then believe on the basis of the works you have seen me do (cf. John 5:36). Nicodemus had correctly seen that no one could do these works without the power of God in him (John 3:2), and similar judgments had been made about Jesus' healings (John 9:33; 10:21). Although Jesus rejected an approach to his mission that would overwhelm by miracle and compel belief (cf. Matt. 4:1–11), he did see the works as confirming evidence that should help.

Jesus then gave what must have been astounding words to Philip and all the disciples (including James) when he said that believers will do works like his and indeed greater ones (vv. 12–14). Jesus had been constrained (cf. Luke 12:50) to the limitation of his earthly body and the Palestinian locale, but they will do greater works in terms of quantity and breadth as he sends them out into all the world (John 17:20; Matt. 28:19). These works they will accomplish because Jesus goes to the Father and because he sends his Spirit to them (v. 16). Whatever they ask in his name he will do. The operative phrase here is "in my name," for it hedges out all selfish and foolish askings and sets the matter in the context of God-directed prayer: "Not my will but thine be done" (Mark 14:36). If the believer prays in the context of the will of God in this way, that prayer Jesus will answer. It is in light of this power and this assurance that Philip and James and the others went out into all the world, extending the work of Christ in such fashion that Paul would say of the church, "You are the body of Christ" (1 Cor. 12:27).

HOMILETICAL INTERPRETATION

First Lesson: Isa. 30:18–21. In this lesson the preacher may want to reflect on the difficulty of waiting patiently for God's justice to come in an unjust world. Both the psalm for the day (Ps. 44) and the prophetic word call us to faithfulness in difficult times.

Perhaps the most productive approach for today's festival will be that of expanding upon the new day when words of hope and comfort for the future will be heard again and when "the teachers" will be heeded. These teachers will act as the voice of conscience directing the people on the right path, or way. In light of the early church we remember their designation as "followers of the Way" (Acts 9:2). Philip, James, and the others were those who proclaimed Christ as "the Way, the Truth, and the Life" (see Gospel). What is needed today is not a new revelation or a new theophany but guidance on the straight and narrow path that leads to salvation.

Second Lesson: 2 Cor. 4:1–6. Here Paul speaks about the manner of going about the task of mission work. He defends his office, and by implication that of Philip and James, indicating that he uses no trickery or shortcuts. It is a temptation in all ages to package or peddle the Word in such fashion as to win converts at all costs. When the tide of religion goes out and all manner of sects and fringe movements seem to have success, the church needs to be reminded to hold fast to the central truths of the gospel. The masses may have "itching ears" for teachers of their own liking and reject sound teaching (2 Tim. 4:3), but to tamper with the message and give what the market demands will yield only superficial gains and no long-term fruit.

A second line of approach in this lesson might be to focus on the light image, the light that the darkness of ignorance and opposition cannot put out (John 1:5). It is, as Paul writes, this light that we hold up, not ourselves. Those who are on the Way seek the light and not the darkness (1 John 1:7).

Gospel: John 14:8–14. Our three lessons come into united focus in this text. Jesus is the expected Way, the undistorted Truth, and the illuminating Life. It is to this that Philip and James and the rest of us bear witness.

Like Philip, many among us seek new revelations and confirmations of our faith in God in a world filled with death-of-God talk and with the dark clouds of apathy and disbelief. The preacher may well emphasize that in Christ we have seen a vision of the Father sufficient for salvation. What the world needs now is not a new vision and a new theology but the extension of that culminating vision in the loving lives of Christian witnesses.

Another thrust of the text hinges on the doing of greater works than even Jesus did. We modern disciples have the opportunity, and the challenge, to extend Jesus' ministry worldwide. Here one may employ the media and all manner of new missionary strategies and technologies to advance the kingdom. The key to success, however, will still be prayer "in his name" and the empowering Holy Spirit. Theology must still be lord over technology. No matter how great the budget, how enthusiastic the witnesses, how sophisticated the technology, it is a fearful thing to be the body of Christ by our own wit and resources. In the context of his will and Spirit, it is indeed the only Way and our right path in today's world. Those who advance this Way may not be luminaries like Peter or Paul, or even lesser lights like Stephen and James "the less," but it is upon their shoulders that the kingdom comes, and they are known by name to God.

The Visitation

MAY 31

Lutheran	Roman Catholic	Episcopal
Isa. 11:1–5	Zeph. 3:14–18	Zeph. 3:14–18a
Rom. 12:9–16	Rom. 12:9–16	Col. 3:12–17
Luke 1:39–47	Luke 1:39–56	Luke 1:39–49

EXEGESIS

First Lesson: Isa. 11:1–5. This text should be read in connection with Isa. 9:2–7. Although the term "Messiah" does not appear, the passage is clearly messianic, as may be seen by comparison of the elements here with Psalm 72. This psalm, together with other coronation or royal psalms (cf. Pss. 2; 45; 132; 145, for example), extols the virtues of the true king and expresses hope that this coronation (cf. 2 Kings 11:12) will bring in the ideal king and kingdom. No earthly king fulfilled this hope or the depth of the promise to the house of David (2 Sam. 7:4–17). The expectation grew to the exalted phraseology of Isaiah 9.

V. 1 conveys the notion that the Davidic house is weakened, if not in fact cut down. Just as David was chosen from humble origins in the house of Jesse (1 Sam. 16:1–13; 2 Sam. 7:18) to become king, so a new shoot or root will appear, a second David. Although the Hebrew terms used are not identical, the notion is akin to the prophetic hope for a righteous Branch (Jer. 23:5; 33:15; Zech. 3:8; 6:12; and Isa. 4:2).

His faith and source of strength are described in vv. 2 and 3a. Just as the life-giving Spirit was with David (1 Sam. 16:13), so this new Davidic ruler will be empowered. Like Solomon, he will have the gifts of wisdom and understanding to "deal wisely" (Jer. 23:5). Having the Spirit of counsel and might, he will not need to depend upon human advisors, nor will he lack the ability to put these decisions into action. Furthermore, he will have the twin virtues of true piety: knowledge of God (cf. Hos. 4:1) and reverence for God, which is the fountainhead of all wisdom (cf. Prov. 1:7). One major burden of Hosea's message was that the priests and leaders did not impart knowledge of God, and that although the people protested that they knew God (Hos. 8:2), they knew only about him but did not know him personally and intimately, thus falling into sin and error (Hos. 4:1ff.). This ideal king will indeed know and revere God.

Vv. 3b through 5 speak of the fruits of such royal Spirit as expressed in his actions as God's king. He will not judge like other earthly kings, by appearances and hearsay (v. 3b), but will exercise judgment with righteousness (cf. 2 Sam. 23:3), even, or especially, when dealing with the poor and the oppressed—always the objects of special conern in the OT law (cf. Exod. 22:21–22; Deut. 27:19, etc.).

This righteous king will deal decisively in judgment on those who break the covenant; he shall slay the wicked (v. 4). The administration of the true king will include compassion for the weak and punishment for oppressors. The aura of his office will be not pomp and circumstance but righteousness and faithfulness.

Both the Roman Catholic and Episcopal First Lessons focus on Zeph. 3:14–18 (or 18a). Here the prophet announces salvation and calls the "daughter of Zion" to sing in joy for the coming King. On this day we celebrate the new daughter of Zion, Mary, who sings in joy over the coming King of the new Israel.

Second Lesson: Rom. 12:9–16. The Book of Romans turns from a complex and sustained theological discourse to the practical matters of the Christian life with the famous "therefore" in 12:1. Just as Paul moves from the varieties of Christian gifts (1 Cor. 12) to his homily on love (1 Cor. 13), so he moves here from a discussion of the variety of gifts (Rom. 12:1–8), with an exhortation to their application, to our text which involves the practical working out of love in the Christian community (12:9–16 and indeed on to 21). Whereas believers may share only one or some of the gifts, all should express these traits in community life.

The connection with today's festival may be seen in the mixture of prayer, humility, and devotion of Mary with commitment to dealing with the lowly, caring for human needs, or social action, as expressed in her song (Luke 1:46–55). Mary expresses much of the ideal life of the community urged here.

Paul calls for a genuine love, agape, as expanded upon in 1 Corinthians 13, reflective of the very love of God (1 John 4). Believers are to hate evil (Ps. 97:10) and to express brotherly affection (Heb. 13:1), as in the sharing of gifts for the needy (1 Thess. 4:9). In humility one is to honor others (1 Pet. 2:17), accounting them more important than oneself (Phil. 2:3).

With regard to diligence, one is not to be slothful (cf. Prov. 6:6). The phrase rendered "never flag in zeal" in the RSV probably reflects the expressly Christian tasks in which one should not "grow weary" (Gal. 6:9). With regard to the spirit, one is to be "fervent," or better, "boiling hot" (cf. Rev. 3:15). This fervor of spirit was characteristic of the apostles at their best (Acts 18:25). The zeal and fervor are summed up in the injunction to serve (be the servant or slave of) the Lord.

The Christian rejoices in hope (Rom. 5:2 and expanded upon in 1 Pet. 1:3–9), is patient in "tribulation" or oppression and affliction, not only in the Tribulation to come but in sufferings common to the cause (John 16:33). One is enabled to be hopeful and patient because of the steadfastness or constancy of prayer (Col. 4:2; 1 Thess. 5:17) so often exhibited in the early church (Acts 6:1–4, etc.).

Concern for others is not a matter of the heart only but involves the making of contributions for the needy (for example 1 Cor. 16:1ff. and many other places) and entails practicing or pursuing hospitality (cf. Matt. 25:35 and Heb. 13:2).

Paul, like Jesus (Luke 6:28; Matt. 5:44), calls for blessing one's persecutors, as Jesus did from the cross (Luke 23:34). The disciples are to relate to one another in appropriate responses as the unified body of Christ, rejoicing or weeping as the circumstances dictate. This empathetic emotional response is a manifestation of the harmony to which the disciples are called, "thinking the same thing to one another" ("live in harmony"), which Paul discusses later (15:5). Peter expresses it as having unity of spirit, sympathy, and love (1 Pet. 3:8). Paul uses the same expression for harmony and adds that it expresses having the mind of Christ in the group (Phil. 2:2, 5).

Finally, the apostle warns against being haughty or proud (cf. Ps. 131:1) and urges "going along with" or "association" with the lowly (cf. 1 Tim. 6:1–2; James 2:1–7). In summary he says, "Do not be wise in yourselves" ("conceited"), as he had warned earlier (Rom. 11:25). Throughout this catalog of expressions of the Christian life, the devout are warned not to turn in on themselves but to look to the needs of others.

Gospel: Luke 1:39–47. The psalm for today (113) is particularly apt for the study of this text. In that psalm God is praised and blessed for his glory above and for his saving acts on behalf of the poor and needy below. Especially noted is the joy of the barren woman who has a child (v. 9)—a verse pregnant with meaning for Elizabeth, whose joy is twofold: for her own son and for the coming of the Messiah. Both Elizabeth and Mary "praise the Lord" (Ps. 113:9) because of the uniqueness of their pregnancies.

Our text culminates with the utterance of the Magnificat (so named from the Latin Vulgate) and is shot through with OT allusions, parallels, and quotations.

Mary quickly went to visit her kinswoman Elizabeth after the annunciation and, we presume, the virginal conception of Jesus. She traveled to the unnamed city in Judah (cf. 1:23) to the house of Zechariah and greeted Elizabeth. More than simply saying "hello" is implied—Mary relates the account of the angel's visit and words. Upon hearing all this, Elizabeth's child leaped for joy (cf. v. 44), an expression used uniquely by Luke (cf. 6:23) and reminiscent of Rebekah's struggling twins (Gen. 25:22). Just as it had been said that John would be filled with the Holy Spirit from his mother's womb (1:15), so Elizabeth is inspired.

Elizabeth cries out that Mary is blessed among women (cf. Ruth in

Ruth 3:10 and Jael in Judg. 5:24, both of whom are deemed blessed for their faithful action). Mary's blessed estate is not due to her understanding of her Son's person and work, for she and the family had difficulty understanding it (Luke 2:50; Mark 3:21, 31–35). In response to a woman who later declared Jesus' mother to be blessed, Jesus counters with the affirmation that blessedness comes from hearing and doing the word of God (Luke 11:27–28). In fact, whoever does the will of God, Jesus says, is brother, sister, or mother to him (Mark 3:31–35). One may well recall the blessings in Deut. 28:3ff. which flow to those who obey the Lord. Mary is blessed by God for her trusting obedience. There is nothing in the text to suggest that she herself is a repository of this grace or blessing to dispense it to others. Together with the faithful mother, the unborn Jesus is blessed.

In v. 43 Elizabeth responds to this exciting revelation of the presence of God in their midst with classic Jewish pious humility: Why has this been revealed to me? One thinks of Isaiah's humility and confession of sin when granted a vision of God (Isa. 6).

Elizabeth amplifies on the reason for Mary's blessedness—namely, that she had believed that the Lord would fulfill the promise announced. This stands in stark contrast to the response of Elizabeth's husband, Zechariah, who doubted when the announcement had come that previously barren Elizabeth would bear a son (1:18–20). Mary had also questioned how the birth could be, but she had yielded to it and believed. Here we recall the words in John's Gospel speaking of the blessedness of those who have not seen, yet who believe (John 20:29).

There is a debate as to whether vv. 46–55 are spoken by Mary (as most texts and translations render it) or by Elizabeth. The parallels to Hannah's psalm of praise (1 Sam. 1:11; 2:1–10) would fit Elizabeth's situation better than that of Mary, and "her" in v. 56 seems to suggest that Elizabeth was the speaker. On the side of the majority of manuscripts, Mary would be the object of v. 48b—indicating that just as Elizabeth had blessed her, all generations will so do. We take this to be Mary's psalm, reflecting a veritable collage of texts (Ps. 34:2–3; 1 Sam. 2:1–10; Ps. 113, and others). Mary's whole person (soul and spirit) praises God and rejoices. The rest of the poem speaks almost of revolution in God's action on behalf of the poor and downtrodden, actions expressed in the past tense not only because of the prior saving actions of God but also because God's decisive action in Christ has already begun.

With such heavy references to the OT throughout the text, it may be in order to suggest that in v. 56 we have an allusion to the sojourn of the ark of God. David brought up the ark, symbol of the very presence of God (Num. 10:35), and it stayed with Obed-edom for three months before moving into Jerusalem, to Zion. So Mary, filled with the very presence of God, sojourns three months in a Judean household before moving with the ultimate manifestation of "God with us" toward Jerusalem.

HOMILETICAL INTERPRETATION

First Lesson: Isa. 11:1–5. The exalted language of this messianic text reminds us of the ages of frustration with the enthronement and subsequent failure of every earthly king to measure up to this standard. It requires little imagination to draw modern parallels to campaign promises and popular expectations which fail to materialize in new political administrations. Every king was anointed and thus a "messiah" (from *mashiach,* "anointed"), but as hopes grew the concept grew to a capital M, the Messiah. The celebration in the Zephaniah text of God in our midst to save and renew in love was but a foretaste of the Messiah who would fulfill the Davidic office from the divine and not only the human side.

The description of the charismatic gifts of the Messiah in our passage includes intellectual ones (wisdom and understanding), practical ones (counsel and might), and pious ones (knowledge and fear of the Lord). Whereas former kings had fallen short, this one would truly understand our situation, be able to do something about it, and act with model piety. The reign of this king will issue in righteousness, justice, and faithfulness. The preacher will want to apply these gifts and this kingdom not only to Jesus but also to his followers, who should exercise those same gifts of the Spirit and thus show forth the power of such a kingdom.

Second Lesson: Rom. 12:9–16. Our Romans text follows this train of thought as Paul moves from his theological reflection on the person and work of this Messiah to the responsive life of the Christian community. His words recall the fundamentals of the Ten Commandments, now expressed concretely in commonplace virtues and actions. The gifts he listed should issue in the righteousness, justice, and faithfulness of the messianic kingdom. The loving and faithful response of Mary to the announcement of the kingdom's Messiah should be the response of the faithful in every age.

The preacher may focus upon the element of this passage which appears in Mary's song in the Gospel: concern for the poor and lowly. Furthermore, in Mary's humility and responsive faithfulness there is a model for those who in humility will love and serve. Especially powerful is the injunction to respond member-to-member as the body of Christ, weeping with those who weep and rejoicing with those who rejoice. As the women in the Gospel rejoice together, so we imagine their weeping together later at the pain their two sons will occasion. The church sorely needs this empathetic, compassionate response. Can we not point out the pastoral implications of sharing one another's seasons of joy? Can we not underscore the value of the ministry of presence even if we bring only tears and not apt words in our times of sorrow and tears?

The notion here of meeting human needs and showing hospitality moves beyond merely good stewardship practices to the openness of the worshiping community to strangers and sojourners—to the ever-present visitors and newcomers in our midst in this transient society.

Gospel: Luke 1:39–47. Luke's account deals on the surface with Mary and Elizabeth but more substantially with the two sons hidden in their wombs. At a still deeper level the text deals with the impending action of God through John's preparing and Jesus' fulfilling ministries. Just as at this time of the year new growth is bursting forth about us, so God's new thing in Christ is about to burst forth through these hope-filled pregnancies.

One powerful theme here is the contrast of the humble and faithful Mary with the doubting Zechariah. So too we moderns are more filled with questions than affirmations, dumb to the world when it comes to expressing that which is a stumbling block or folly to the pragmatic world in which we live. In contrast to Mary, who yields to God, we fail to expect God to do mighty things in our midst. Perhaps we need a reminder that God wills to act through even the likes of us, not in our power but in our humble weakness. As Paul would say again and again, "When I am weak, then I am strong" (2 Cor. 12:10). When in humility we will allow ourselves to be used by God, even though we know in our frailty that we are but "earthen vessels" (2 Cor. 4:7), God's saving power comes to us and through us to others.

St. Barnabas, Apostle

JUNE 11

Lutheran	Roman Catholic	Episcopal
Isa. 42:5–12		Isa. 42:5–12
Acts 11:19–30; 13:1–3	Acts 11:21–26; 13:1–3	Acts 11:19–30; 13:1–3
Matt. 10:7–16	Matt. 10:7–13	Matt. 10:7–16

Although not one of the Twelve, Barnabas was called an apostle by the early church fathers. Tradition has it that he was one of the seventy (Luke 10:1), and the Anglican calendar designates him as "apostle"—the only one outside of Paul and the evangelists to be so honored. He was born in Cyprus but doubtless had connections in Jerusalem, John Mark being his cousin. With his Hellenist background he was a logical choice for the extension of the gospel to the Gentiles, and he pleaded their case in the Jerusalem council (Acts 15), although something of the old Jewish spirit remained in him (cf. Gal. 2:13). He was accounted "a good man, full of the Holy Spirit and of faith" (Acts 11:24), with apparent gifts as a reconciler. The feast honoring him was designated by St. Charles Borromeo at the Sixth Council in 1582.

EXEGESIS

First Lesson: Isa. 42:5–12. Our text follows immediately after one of the servant songs (42:1–4); however, most scholars agree that this is an independent unit. We interpret this passage as referring not to Cyrus, nor to an individual servant, but rather to Israel. Here Deutero-Isaiah deals with God's intervention in Israel's salvation history, a covenant history of significance not only for Israel but for all the nations. It is a "new song" set in the context of God's action and intention in all creation.

V. 5 is an expansion on the common prophetic introductory formula "thus saith the Lord," detailing who this Lord is. It is a hymn to the Creator (cf. Isa. 40:12–14; 43:1, et al. for the stress on the Creator). The Lord has not only created, in the metalworker imagery beating out the heavens and the earth, but he has been and is the source of the very essence of life, the breath and spirit of all that lives.

The section 6 through 9 deals with the nature of Israel's calling and their task in God's salvation history. The God who created has also personally and in righteousness redeemed. Israel has been grasped by the hand and kept by God, a calling not for themselves alone but for all humankind. The phrase "a covenant to the people" is unusual (cf. 49:8) but becomes clear in parallel to "a light to the nations." Israel's covenant is for all humankind, just as Abraham's call was to be a blessing to all (Gen. 12:3). Throughout Israel's checkered history the "grasping" of God in special covenant relationship was distorted into a matter of national pride and self-interest; at its prophetic best, however, it was understood as a calling to a task: to serve and witness to the nations. The specific tasks here listed, giving sight to the blind and bringing out prisoners, imply a spiritual task much broader than dealing with the blindness of Zedekiah and imprisonment of Jehoiachin (cf. Isa. 35:5–6; 61:1). These covenantal salvific tasks are taken up by Jesus (cf. Matt. 11:5).

Vv. 8 and 9 remind the hearers of the name and nature of God, "I am" (cf. Exod. 3:14), and of the covenantal response of giving him alone the glory and praise, praise not due to idols of Babylon or any other. This "new thing" of God's salvation bursts forth like flowers after the early rains.

The final two double-verse strophes call again for the joyous singing response to God's action (cf. Pss. 33:3; 96:1; 98:1; 149:1). Just as Miriam sang her song of joy in response to God's salvation in the exodus event (Exod. 15:21), so now all peoples far and near and indeed all creation are summoned into such joyous song. Specific identification of Kedar as Arab tribes and Sela as Petra are difficult but not important for the text, as they are simply cases in point of all peoples responding in universal praise. The eschatological hymn of praise indicates that the proper response of all creation is to give glory and praise to God.

Second Lesson: Acts 11:19–30; 13:1–3. Our text picks up on "those who were scattered" (Acts 8:4) after the death of Stephen. Some had come to Antioch and a church had sprung up there. At first the gospel was announced to Jews only (v. 19), but then some Cypriots and Cyrenians spoke to Greeks as well. There is some debate as to whether these were Hellenists (Greek-speaking Jews) or Hellenes (Greeks). As the passage and the missionary movement clearly imply, this was an extension of the gospel to Greeks, to pagans. This reference to previously unknown and unauthorized missionary work probably reflects the pattern of lay Christians spreading all over the Roman Empire.

As the hand of the Lord moved mightily in the OT (cf. Exod. 8:19; 14:31, for example), so their proclamation had the divine sanction (as in Acts 4:30; 13:11). Further confirmation of their good work was in the numbers coming to faith.

Conscious of their seniority and feeling a sense of responsibility for the spread of the church throughout the world, the church at Jerusalem sent Barnabas to Antioch to investigate the matter. He was a wise choice, a Cypriot Jew who might be well received. He is described as a "good man," gracious and kindly, "full of the Holy Spirit and of faith" (v. 24; cf. Stephen in Acts 6:5). Barnabas was impressed with the work of the lay missionaries at Antioch and saw in it the grace of God. Employing the gift of exhortation (Rom. 12:8) he urged that they hold fast to the faith.

Barnabas, meaning "son of encouragement or consolation," received his Christian name (Acts 4:36) shortly after his conversion, even as Paul had received his new name Paul. Prior to that (Acts 13:9) Paul was still referred to as Saul, though we shall use the name Paul throughout this discussion.

The church grew in numbers (v. 24), and Barnabas, who had introduced Paul to the apostles (Acts 9:27), sought out Paul to come and labor with him. The two shared a congenial and successful ministry for a year in Antioch and subsequent mission work to the Gentiles together. Unfortunately Paul and Barnabas later had a painful break and parted company (Acts 15:39–40).

We note with interest that the disciples in Antioch were the first to be called Christians—possibly a derisive nickname (see the mocking usage in Acts 26:28), or perhaps simply stating that they were "of Christ's party" as the Herodians were "of Herod's party" (Matt. 22:16). In any event, the term was an apt and useful one in that it joined the diverse mix of Jews and pagans under the one name, a name that quickly became one of honor (1 Pet. 4:16).

Vv. 27–30 tell of the prophetic words of Agabus announcing an extensive famine and of the generosity of the church in making an offering for the poor in Judea. The elders of the church sent that offering by the hand of Barnabas and Paul—the order of names implying that Barnabas was the more distinguished of the two at the time. Barnabas must have been an impressive figure, for at Lystra he was identified with Zeus, or Jupiter, whereas Paul was deemed to be Hermes, or Mercury (Acts 14:12). It was well-known that Barnabas was committed to the sharing of worldly possessions for the life of the church. After his conversion he sold a field which belonged to him and turned over the money to the apostles (Acts 4:37). Thus it is fitting that he should be involved in this ministry of communicating the offering to those in need.

In Acts 13:1–3 we see the cosmopolitan mix of the Antioch church, mother to gentile Christianity. Here the prophets and teachers amongst the membership composed something like an executive committee for the work of the church. It is clear that they were worshiping with prayer and fasting, waiting for the inspiration of the Holy Spirit (cf. Luke 5:35). The leading of the Spirit caused the elders to give a special commissioning to Barnabas and Paul, who were "set apart" for their missionary work. Just as the Levites (Num. 16:9) and Aaron (1 Chron. 23:13) were set apart, so Paul describes himself (Rom. 1:1; Gal. 1:15). This was not an ordination to ministry as an initiation rite but a special commissioning service.

Gospel: Matt. 10:7–16. Our text does not deal with Barnabas, who does not appear in the Gospels, but with the instructions given to the Twelve when they were sent out by Jesus. It is clear that these instructions would apply equally well to those, such as Barnabas, who would follow in Christian ministry.

This account is given also in Mark (6:8–11) and in Luke (9:1–5) with some minor variations: Mark and Luke do not prohibit wearing sandals; only Matthew mentions raising from the dead. The overall thrust is common to the synoptics: the Twelve are sent forth to extend the work of Jesus, doing the things which he had done, and they are to go without elaborate preparation and concern for temporal things. So it would be for Barnabas and others later.

They were to go preaching (the kerygma word) that "the kingdom of heaven is at hand," as John the Baptist (Matt. 3:2) and, more importantly, Jesus had done (Matt. 4:17). Implicit in that proclamation would be the call for repentance, as in the case of both Jesus and John.

The apostles, "sent ones," were also to duplicate and extend the saving actions of Jesus recounted by Matthew (chaps. 8 and 9) in healing the sick, raising the dead, cleansing the lepers, and casting out demons. As they had been given salvation freely themselves, they were to seek no pay for this work.

Though they were not to earn wages as ministers, they were not to waste time and energy on temporal provisions either. The instruction is to travel light and let the hearers provide for their needs. This instruction may be likened to that regarding the manna in the wilderness: the manna would be sufficiently provided by the Lord day by day and was not to be accumulated, like gaining wealth (cf. Exod. 16:13–21). Thus the Twelve were not to take money, traveling bags, and clothes, for they deserved to be provided for—"the laborer is worth his food" (Luke calls it "his pay" in Luke 10:7). It is interesting in this connection to notice 1 Cor. 9:3–14, where Paul applies this instruction to himself and to Barnabas, contending that Peter and the other apostles are having their temporal needs met whereas only he and Barnabas must engage in a tent-making ministry, that is, must provide for their own needs contrary to Jesus' instruction. In this passage Paul clearly says that the Lord has instructed that "those who proclaim the gospel should get their living by the gospel" (1 Cor. 9:14). It is quite evident from this text that such things did not always work out easily and were particularly problematic for Barnabas and for Paul.

When going about their ministry, the apostles were to show the common courtesy of saluting the house (Matt. 5:47), having selected only "worthy" houses to stay in. The word "worthy" (*axia*) connotes being deserving or fit, as in being "worthy" of one's food (10:10). Luke renders this episode by saying that one should extend the peace and if there are "sons of peace" there, then the apostle should reside there (Luke 10:6). It appears that in this case it is not so much a matter of the householders' being righteous or "worthy" in themselves but of their being in tune with the message, being expectant, or being receptive. If the chosen house proved not to be worthy, the blessing given was to revert to the itinerant preacher. There is a sense of haste and urgency about their work. If people will not receive them (not take them into their homes) or will not listen, they are to shake off the dust of their sandals, a symbolic act of rejection (Acts 13:51 and similar acts in Neh. 5:13; Acts 18:6). Similar issues are at work in the epistles of John where there is a warning not to receive into the house or give any greeting to those who are heretics, not holding sound doctrine (2 John 10–11), lest one be implicated in their wickedness; there is also a reproof of Diotrephes, who judged incorrectly in this matter and refused to show hospitality to some of the brethren (3 John 9–10). It was not easy then—nor is it now—to separate the wheat from the tares, to know the true preachers when hearing them. The judgment on those who reject the apostles is quite severe in our text: it will be better for Sodom and Gomorrah, those bywords of iniquity (Gen. 18—19), in the last days.

Finally, Jesus says, the work of the apostles is dangerous and serious—they are like sheep among wolves. They are enjoined to be as wise, or prudent and sensible, as serpents but to be as harmless as doves (v. 16). Theirs was a perilous task, and foolish risks should not be taken, but they were not to repay evil for evil and become like the wolves.

HOMILETICAL INTERPRETATION

First Lesson: Isa. 42:5–12. Here the preacher may settle in on the concept of God's calling or choosing his people. Those called are selected not for privilege but for service. God works through his people not for their good only but for their covenantal witness and mission on behalf of all humanity. The servant role for Israel and for the new Israel entails specific acts of compassion in medical work (healing) and prison ministry (both visitation to and liberation of captives). God's reach to us demands outreach. The church needs to hear again the servant task, which both Jesus and the early church took up. The church needs to know that the "I Am" covenanting God calls his covenant people not only to devotion and the rejection of false idolatries in worship but to acts of loving service among the handicapped (blind) and the socially outcast (prisoners). Let the preacher of this word resist an easy spiritualizing of this mission into merely intellectual illumination and spiritual release from guilt. Let the call to concrete deeds of mercy be clear.

The work of the modern Barnabas, son of encouragement, will so console and encourage the world that new songs of praise and glory to God will be sung by all creation. The intention of this servant ministry is the wholeness or salvation of the whole world which "God so loved" that he sent his servant Son (John 3:16).

Second Lesson: Acts 11:19–30; 13:1–3. The Acts text carries this theme further as we see the expansion of the church beyond the chosen Jews to the whole gentile world. Here one may note with joy and thanksgiving to the empowering Spirit that evangelization and expansion do not always come by church programs and designed campaigns but often by providentially random witnessing by those scattered about the world. We need to look beyond the parochialism of our programs and institutions and like Barnabas perceive what may be happening by the grace of God around us. We need to link up with and make common cause with those ventures whereby the church is advancing, rather than rejecting Christian developments or movements which do not bear our denominational stamp or institutional imprimatur.

The preacher may want to celebrate the concern of the Jerusalem church (the "sending" or main-line church?) for these new Christians, but let him or her take care not to appear patronizing in this oversight of them. Barnabas, as reconciler, gently and appreciatively handled this situation and made helpful common cause with the work going on in Antioch.

This text may give occasion to celebrate the name Christian which we bear. It may have been a term of mocking first, but what higher tribute could we have than to be called "little Christs"? Would anyone accuse us of that? Let us celebrate this inclusive term which encompasses Jew and Gentile, male and female, slave and free, Baptist and Lutheran, Pentecostal and Presbyterian.

Another line of approach would be to discuss the seriousness of

commitment and support evidenced in the special commissioning of
Paul and Barnabas to this work (Acts 13:1-3). With the piety of prayer
and fasting and with the communal act of laying on of hands we
devote, or set apart, persons with special commissions to act on
behalf of the whole church in particular service.

Gospel: Matt. 10:7-16. In the instructions to the Twelve, the
church is called anew to the extension of the work of Jesus. Here we
may appropriately discuss the whole matter of recompense and pro-
fessional service in ministry. There is clear warning that this service
should not be simply a means of gaining material possessions. (Cf.
Amaziah's view that the prophetic office was simply a job, a means of
"earning bread"—Amos 7:12.) But at the same time those who are set
apart to this work should not be distracted from it by worrying about
food, clothing, and shelter. The remuneration should free a Barnabas
to be about the task of ministry with undivided attention. A theology
of pastoral ministry is implicit here. Can some grumbling about
pastoral salaries and church overhead be put in perspective here?

Unfortunately many people are worried about their personal
worthiness. They are concerned not only about whether they are
worthy to be pastors or worthy to come to the Lord's table but also
about whether they are worthy to hear the gospel and to bear the name
Christian. Discussion of Jesus' teachings here about those who are
worthy to host the Twelve and about the shaking off the sandals
against the unworthy is important. The worthiness here, as the
exegesis indicated, is that of being receptive and open to the message.
The writer of Hebrews noted that many witnesses were martyred and
rejected, of whom "the world was not worthy" (Heb. 11:38). The
concern is whether one is receptive, expectant, and open to the
gospel, not whether there is an inner worthiness or righteousness.
Christ came to sinners and can "give sight" to those who know they
are blind. The unworthy ones are those who think that in their own
power they see (John 9:41).

Finally, there is once again a reminder that there was, is, and will be
vicious opposition to the kingdom and to those who announce its
coming. The image of God's people as a flock, as his sheep, abounds
in Scripture. These sheep are in a threatening world but are called to
gentleness among these wolves. The ability to resist becoming wolf-

like and to endure persecution comes in knowing that "the Lord is my shepherd" (Ps. 23) and that the Good Shepherd (Ezek. 34 and John 10) is with us even unto the end of the age—even in the twentieth century.

The Nativity of St. John the Baptist

JUNE 24

Lutheran	Roman Catholic	Episcopal
Mal. 3:1–4	Isa. 49:1–6	Isa. 40:1–11
Acts 13:13–26	Acts 13:22–26	Acts 13:14b–26
Luke 1:57–67 (68–80)	Luke 1:57–66, 80	Luke 1:57–80

EXEGESIS

First Lesson: Mal. 3:1–4. This text should be read as a response to the well-nigh blasphemous raising of the problem of evil in Mal. 2:17. There the people have wearied, and probably angered, the Lord by raising the old theological chestnut of why the wicked prosper (cf. Habakkuk, Job, and Ps. 73 for example)—even challenging God by asking, "Where is the God of justice?"

The prophet, whose name, Malachi, means "my messenger," announces an oracle from God indicating that he will send his messenger to prepare the way for his coming. The old messengers, the priests, had failed (2:7). Now God will send his own messenger or angel (cf. Judg. 13:3) who will prepare the way even as the Second Isaiah had earlier announced (Isa. 40:3). Subsequent to this preparation the Lord will suddenly appear in his temple (cf. Isa. 6). They have asked for the God of justice (2:17), and he whom they seek will appear. Just as the people had yearned for the coming of the Day of the Lord only to be told by Amos that such a day would bring judgment (Amos 5:18–20), so Malachi indicates that when this one they seek does come they will be in for a painful cleansing. His manifestation will be reminiscent of the coming of the Lord in the great theophany of Sinai

(Exod. 19 and 20). Such theophanies were seen, especially by the Priestly writer, as coming through intermediaries or angels of the covenant rather than face-to-face. The passage here suggests that the forerunner or first messenger prepares the temple for the full and immediate coming of the Lord himself.

V. 2 continues the thought of the painful cleansing, asking who can stand in such a day (cf. Ps. 130:3). The cleansing is expressed by the piling up of verbs denoting refining, purging, and purifying. The images of metal being refined by fire until the dross is extracted, and of cloth being beaten about in soapy water until impurities are removed, suggest not a total destruction but a painfully thorough purging which will leave a purified remnant—a motif well-known in the prophet Isaiah. The purging will begin with the Levites, the priests, under whom the evils had been documented (1:6—2:9). After such preparation they will present right offerings (cf. Ps. 4:5), not lame and sick animals (1:8, 13). Just as their prayers are sweet to the Lord (cf. Ps. 104:34; 141:2), so will purified and right sacrifices be. The devotion of the prepared and purified people will be acceptable to God as it was in "the good old days" (cf. Jer. 2:2–3; Mal. 2:6).

The Roman Catholic First Lesson is Isa. 49:1–6, a servant song, in which the servant was seen to be called from the womb (cf. Luke 1:15). Just as the servant feared that his work was in vain (v. 4), so John doubted the effect of his ministry as he languished in prison (Matt. 11:2–6). John, like the servant, was comforted with the task of being a witness to the light to the nations, preparing for the Christ who would be that light (cf. John 1:6–8).

The Episcopal First Lesson is from Second Isaiah, Isa. 40:1–11. This word of comfort announces the end of exile and judgment and sets the tone for the new exodus in that prophet's thought. John the Baptist would also herald the new saving acts of God and would specifically be viewed as "the voice of one crying in the wilderness" (Luke 3:4). Although the Isaiah text reads, "the voice of one crying: in the wilderness prepare . . . ," the sense of continuity and of fulfillment in John's wilderness ministry is clear.

Second Lesson: Acts 13:13–26. The Book of Acts turns from the emphasis on Peter in chaps. 1—12 to the missionary labors of Paul in chap. 13. According to the South Galatian theory, Paul's Letter to the Galatians was addressed to the flocks in Antioch, Iconium, Lystra,

and Derbe. This would be the account of Paul's beginning work there.
Paul emerged as the leader of the enterprise (cf. Acts 9:15) despite
the seniority of Barnabas. John Mark left Paul for reasons which are
the subject of speculation. Suffice it to say that Paul was not pleased
with that development (cf. Acts 15:38). Paul's move to the Gentiles
may have been at issue. Antioch of Pisidia, colony and chief city of
the district of Phrygia, lay in the interior and was reached only by an
arduous trip through the mountains. There Paul went first to the
synagogue. In proper order of worship and with proper authorization
by the rulers of the synagogue, Paul was invited to speak after the
Scripture readings. The texts are not identified. Unlike Jesus who
stood to read the Scriptures and then sat down in the posture of the
teacher to speak to those in the synagogue (Luke 4:16ff.), Paul stands,
motions for quiet, and speaks with great intensity. Here we get the
content of Paul's apostolic preaching, according to Luke, pictured
not unlike that of the other apostles.

Paul addresses the message both to Jews and to the Greeks, "men
of Israel and you that fear God" (v. 16). He gives a historical survey
moving from the patriarchs through the exodus experience, the wilderness, the conquest, the period of the judges, and the kingship,
culminating with the kingship of David. He speaks of the election of
Israel, the saving act in exodus, and the patience of God in "bearing
with" Israel's recalcitrance in the wilderness. It is attractive to read
the latter as "tenderly bearing like a father" (parallel to Deut. 1:31);
however, there is no textual support for the change. Moreover the
emphasis on Israel's scoffing and lack of faith would accord well with
Paul's warning in vv. 40–41.

It is not profitable for us to belabor the "four hundred and fifty
years" Paul cites in v. 19. It probably goes back to Abraham and
carries through Joshua (cf. Gal. 3:17) but at any rate indicates a great
length of time between the promise and the fulfillment in the conquest. It is significant that Paul stresses election and promise, the
saving acts for Israel and through Israel, and omits reference to
covenant and law. His focus later in the sermon will be on the
deliverance wrought by Jesus that frees people as the law of Moses
could not (vv. 38–41).

One should note the emphasis on Samuel, last of the judges and a
prophet, and the coming of kingship in Israel (vv. 20–22). Paul cites
portions of Scripture elevating David (Ps. 89:20 and 1 Sam. 13:14) and

then springs forward to Jesus as seed of David and Savior—implicitly recalling the royal theology in Nathan's promise of one from the house of David who will be established forever (2 Sam. 7:13; see also Ps. 132:11).

Of primary interest to us today is the fact that Paul here explicitly discusses John the Baptist as the forerunner of the Messiah. John preached a baptism of repentance (Mark 1:4). He made no claims for himself but pointed rather to the mightier One to come (Mark 1:7; John 1:20-23; Matt. 3:11; Luke 3:16). As David had been a great king, and promises to him pointed to the greater King to come, so John is a great prophet (cf. Matt. 11:2-15) who points to a greater One yet to come.

In v. 26 Paul returns to the address to Jew and gentile believers alike and announces that "to us," that is, to all people, has been sent the message of this fulfillment which is for our salvation. This note introduces his gospel (vv. 26-37) and subsequent appeal (vv. 38-41).

Gospel: Luke 1:57-67 (68-80). Today's psalm (141) provides a background in fervent prayer for salvation from one's enemies. Particular association with our text in Luke might be made with reference to v. 3, where the psalmist asks the Lord to guard his mouth (cf. Zechariah in Luke 1:20, 22, and 64).

Luke has skillfully woven together the nativity stories of Jesus and of John the Baptist, carefully delimiting John's role and noting the superiority of Jesus. After the mixing of the two stories in the account of Mary's visit, Luke devotes the rest of chap. 1 to John and his parents. We will hear more of John when he begins his public ministry in chap. 3.

Vv. 57-58 indicate that this wondrous happening had not been known even among neighbors and kinsfolk until the birth occurred. They come and congratulate the parents. We learn that they "were calling" the child Zechariah after his father; however, at the time of the circumcision on the eighth day (cf. Lev. 12:3; Gen. 17:12; Phil. 3:5) Elizabeth objects to this name and says he will be called John. That kinfolk might participate in naming is clear (cf. Ruth 4:17). It was unusual for the naming to be connected with circumcision, but so it was for Jesus (2:31). One may recall that Abram was given the new name Abraham at the time of his circumcision as an adult (Gen. 17), and it seems likely that what is being emphasized here is that the names John and Jesus, as that of Abraham, were names given by God. Naming was not done lightly. It expressed something of the faith and hope of the parents. Names related to the character and nature of the one named. John is the shortened form of Jehohanan, meaning "gracious gift of Yahweh."

The supernatural origin of the name is further emphasized in the ensuing debate of the kinsfolk with Elizabeth and in the confirmation given when dumb (and now presumably deaf) Zechariah was asked about it and he wrote on a tablet the name John. That "they all marveled" indicates that it was understood that some supernatural power was at work in both parents arriving at the same name without prior collaboration. Zechariah had been given that name for his son by the angel (1:13), and now that he no longer doubted, his temporary dumbness was removed. That which he spoke was a blessing of God, a happening which struck fear and awe in those who observed it. They perceived that God was at work, expectant fervor was stirred up (cf. Ps. 141), and the happenings attendant to the naming were widely discussed in the region. They questioned what manner of child this would be, for they saw the hand of God at work in John (cf. Ps. 80:17; Acts 11:21, etc.).

Zechariah, like his son and wife, was filled with the Holy Spirit and uttered what is now known as the Benedictus (from the Latin Vulgate rendering). This prophetic poem, like the Magnificat earlier in the chapter, centers on praise and thanksgiving for the approaching salvation. Like the Magnificat, this early Christian hymn is full of scriptural allusions, with only a few verses making it specifically relevant to John (vv. 76–79). This evangelical interpretation of prophecy and psalmody speaks of God's saving acts in history pressing backward through the house of David to promises to Abraham.

In vv. 76–79, focusing on John, Zechariah announces that John is the prophet and forerunner of the Messiah (cf. discussion of Mal. 3 above), that he will speak of the coming redemption and forgiveness of sins, that he will be like the day dawning (Mal. 4:2), and that he will bring light to those in deep darkness (Isa. 9:2). John will fulfill prophetic hopes as the forerunner or new Elijah who prepares the way for the Savior or new David.

V. 80 indicates that the child grew strong in body and spirit and then was in the wilderness until his public ministry began. It is appealing to think that John's retreat was in the pattern of the Essenes known to us at Qumran through the Dead Sea Scrolls. John was indeed ascetic; however, his particular preaching of a baptism of repentance is not part of the Qumran tradition.

HOMILETICAL INTERPRETATION

First Lesson: Mal. 3:1–4. The problem of evil is not unknown among us. Throughout history people have asked why the wicked prosper, why the righteous suffer, why the God of justice does not step in and resolve international crises or the plight of refugees, or even more urgently why their own personal woes and tragedies cannot be reversed. Malachi challenges the people with the notion that they may not be as righteous as they think. A major role of the forerunner, or "John the Baptist," in our day will be that of purging, reforming, and cleansing. Such prophetic words are not always well received but are "in season." Here the preacher may call for repentance and the giving of right offerings in stewardship and in obedience as opposed to our inclination to self-righteousness and a self-seeking piety. Those who regularly go in and out of the temple (church) may mistakenly think that they can easily, almost casually, have fellowship with the God of justice without the rigors of repentance and the discipline of obedience.

Isaiah 40 carries this thought further in that the word of comfort comes to those who have been afflicted and chastened. As the old saying puts it, God wills for us to "afflict the comfortable and comfort the afflicted." There is grace here, but not cheap grace.

The Isaiah 49 text pushes in a different direction. It is a servant song and parallels the calling of John from his mother's womb to be an agent of repentance and of the world's redemption. God's servants wonder from time to time whether their work is effective or in vain. The hope then and now is in the Lord who called and who empowers. Let the preacher affirm that it is not for us to worry about results and effectiveness, but rather to concern ourselves with faithfulness. Let the church know that as servant it does not seek its own glory but that of God.

Second Lesson: Acts 13:13–26. Here we get our only detailed look in Acts at Paul's preaching. Among the apostolic sermons we have, only this one specifically deals with John the Baptist. One key theme of the sermon is the expanding graciousness of God seen in a rehearsal of God's acts from great to greater to greatest. First Saul, then the greater David, then the greatest Jesus. First Samuel, then the greater John, then the greatest Jesus. First limited to the Jews, then expanded to the Gentiles, then ultimately to all the world.

Significant for proclamation is the fact that Paul centers on Christ as Savior. In his account of God's mighty acts he does not center on the law but on the One who fulfilled the law and truly set the people free (vv. 38 and 39). In our proclamation of the kingdom and of repentance, let us not suggest a new law but a prepared heart, readied for salvation. Let the preacher be instructed by the model of John the Baptist: we point not to ourselves but to Jesus. The inclination of people to develop allegiances to the person and work of particular pastors is strong. Remember the divisions in the early church: "I belong to Paul" or "to Apollos" or "to Cephas" (1 Cor. 1:12). John did not strive to win followers for himself but to point to and prepare for Christ. We do not do well to "evangelize" and to develop our church's outreach on the basis of "Come and hear Dr. Williams or Pastor Smith," but rather "Come and share in our church's life of response to Jesus."

Gospel: Luke 1:57–67 (68–80). Again in the Gospel text the superiority of Jesus to John is emphasized; the prophetic daystar on the morning horizon yields to the Sun of Righteousness. One might well develop the theme of the goodness of the light as created by God (Gen. 1:3), the light to those in deep darkness (Isa. 9:2), the light to the nations (Isa. 49:6), this daystar light of John, Jesus as the light of the world (John 8), the endurance of that light (John 1:5), the precious treasure of the light in the face of Christ which we proclaim (2 Cor. 4:6), and the enduring challenge to followers of Christ to be the light (Matt. 5:14–16). As John was a light, so are we. As the source of that light was not in John but in God, so it is with us.

Another provocative theme in our lesson is that of the response of the community in awe and wonder to the coming action of God prefigured in the naming and blessing of young John. Though we disclaim such supernatural leading in the naming of our children, cannot we capture something of the awe, wonder, and expectancy as we welcome such blessed ones into our family of faith? Can we praise and glorify God as we ponder how these new little ones may become bearers of God's light? Surely we can and must surround them with the loving prayers, joyous touches of blessing, and constancy of songs of praise that will be for them a nurturing environment. The child may grow "in the wilderness," but let it start off in the warmth and love of the family of faith. Let the church love and nurture not only in church-school curricula and youth programs but also in the warm touch of prayer, celebration, song, and love.